THE GREATEST COACH OF ALL TIME

"HIS GAME CHANGING PLAYBOOK FOR YOUR COMEBACK"

DARREN TAYLOR

The Greatest Coach of All Time & "His Game Changing Playbook for Your Comeback"

DARREN TAYLOR

Global Outreach Book Publishing

Copyright 2017 Darren Taylor

All rights reserved. In accordance with the U.S. Copyright Act of 1976, the scanning uploading, and electronic sharing of any part of this book with-out the permission of the publisher constitute unlawful piracy and theft of the author's intellectual property. If you would like to use material from the book (other than for review purposes), prior written permission must be obtained by contacting the publisher. Your support of the author's rights are greatly appreciated.

All scripture quotations are taken from the Holy Bible, New International Version or the New Living Translation unless indicated otherwise.

Global Outreach Book Publishing
25344 Wesley Chapel Blvd Suite 103
Lutz, FL 33559
www.globaloutreachbookpublishing.com

Printed in the United States Of America

First Edition: October 2017

Library of Congress data has been applied for.

This book is dedicated to Andrea Taylor, an incredible woman, who my "Life Coach" hooked me up with. We've been married for almost 10 years now, and she is one of the biggest reasons that I feel like I'm the richest man alive. I'm grateful to have her in my life. I was a single father of 3 when she came into our lives. And she was a single mother of 3. She treated my kids as her own, by meeting their needs, and disciplining them when they needed it. Without her, they would not have grown up to be the amazing kids they are today. She has inspired me to become a better man. I would also like to dedicate this book to all 6 of our children, little Darren, Justin, Daniel, Blake, Alanna & Jenna. I'm grateful to have all of them in my life, and honored to have had the opportunity to be a father to Alanna, Jenna, and Blake. They have grown up to be amazing kids who I'm proud to call my own.

Contents

Acknowledgements xi
Introduction xiii

1 Let Me Introduce You to My Coach 1
2 He Wants to Help You to Live Your Dreams 3
3 Who Is the Greatest Coach of All Time? 5
4 He Created the Game and Has Equipped You to Win 8
5 The Greatest "LAST MINUTE" Comeback Ever
   "The Thief on The Cross" 12
6 Life Can Be Here Today and Gone Today 15
7 Jesus Brought Lazarus Back to Life After Being
   Dead For 4 Days 16
8 Rudy!!! Rudy!!! You're More Than Just a Ruettiger!!! 20
9 Some of The All-Star Players Jesus Has Coached 24
10 His Star Quarterback 26
11 Jesus' Players Become Talent Scouts for His Team 29
12 The Benefits of Being Coached by Jesus 31
13 Yesterday Is History, Tomorrow Is a Mystery,
   And Today Is a Gift ...That's Why It's Called "The Present" 36
14 I Did the Fire Walk, But He Walked on Water 37
15 My Grandmother Told Me That Jesus Physically
   Appeared to Her 42

16	We Score Victories in Life by Getting into The Faith Zone	45
17	The Hall of Faith	47
18	He Blesses and Disciplines Those He Loves and Those Who Love Him	49
19	The Party's Over	51
20	From Bitter to Better. Jesus Turned Water into Wine and He Can Turn Your Lemons into Lemonade	54
21	Jesus' Favorite Play Call, is to Go Deep	57
22	Judging Others	61
23	What's the Goal?	63
24	You Have Been Pardoned. Now Leave Your Self-imposed Prison	65
25	It's A Mental Game	68
26	Get into His Groove	69
27	Jesus Likes to Call Audibles	70
28	His Players Are Rich, But They Pretend to Be Poor	72
29	Who Are You Playing the Game For?	73
30	You Can't Earn a Spot on His Team	75
31	The Parable of the Great Banquet	77
32	Two Fingers Pointing Back at Me	80
33	Everyone on His Team Is in The Starting Line Up	81
34	Jesus Withdrew the Payment for Your Entry into the Race from the Blood Bank	83
35	The Eating and Training Plan He Puts His Players On	87
36	To Eat or Not to Eat that is the Question	90
37	He Wants You to Turn Your Tests into Your Testimony	92
38	You Are a Player Coach	94

39	When You Believe, You Receive, But When You Doubt, You Go Without	96
40	The 2-Minute Warning	99
41	How Much Time Is Left on Your Game Clock?	101
42	Thoughts Are Seeds	103
43	How to Stop Sleeping the Time Off Your Game Clock	106
44	You Gotta Have a Dream	108
45	How to Get Your Momentum Back	110
46	You Haven't Got a Prayer	112
47	How Many Times Should You Forgive Someone?	114
48	We Win by Losing	117
49	Jesus Hangs Out with The Tailgaters	119
50	He's Going to Help You Finish the Game	122
51	We ALL Fall Short	124
52	The Earth, Sun, Moon, and Stars	126
53	He Created It All - From Start to Finish	128
54	All or Some?	132
55	Review the Highlight Film in Your Mind, Then Move Forward	135
56	His Players Never Retire	137
57	He Loves Giving His Players Great Gifts	139
58	A Personal Testimony from One of Jesus' Players	142
59	We All Have Our Good Games and Our Bad Games	144
60	Savor the Sweet Victories	146
61	What Station Are You Tuned Into?	148
62	He Chooses the Rejects	149
63	He Doesn't Want You to Get Buff at The Buffet	151

64	He Wants You to Walk Your Talk	153
65	He Wants You to Know the Rules of His Game	155
66	Drifting Down the River of Life	157
67	His Players Don't Drink Gatorade	159
68	He Says You Can Predict Your Own Victory	161
69	All His Players Have Eternal Life Insurance	164
70	The Greatest Commandment	166
71	The Blue Tour Bus	168
72	How To Find His Personalized Game Plan for Your Comeback	170

Acknowledgements

This book is dedicated to all my friends and family members who have been there for me throughout my life… through the good and the bad. My father Daniel, my mother Melody, and my stepfather Peter. My grandmother Helen, my father and mother In-law, Henry and Lynda, my brothers, Landen, Scott & Todd, my brother In-Law Aaron and sister In-Law Krista.

My sisters In-law, Kim, Heather & Anna, my great musical friend Ron, my musical mentor Bobby, my earliest guitar influences, Stevie, Bill and John, and my longtime friend Ed. I would also like to dedicate this book to all the inspiring teachers and coaches throughout my life. Especially Coach Macal. But, above all, I would like to thank and acknowledge my personal "Life Coach Jesus Christ" whom I believe is "The Greatest Coach of All Time."

Introduction

It was 28 to 3 when the band hit the field, it was quiet in that locker room. It's hard to catch your breath when you fight with all your heart, and more than our pride was bruised. But there's a Man with a plan, and fire in His eyes, and He knows how to pull us through.

He said you can't make a sack, or a fifty-yard pass, if you're standing on the side lines. When you get knocked down, and you're out of time outs, you *"gotta"* prove that it's your time. You *"gotta"* play the second half, like the two-minute warning, lay it all on the line. "*Cuz* it *ain't* ever over at Half Time.

Those were the words that I co-wrote at a songwriting session in Nashville, Tennessee, nearly 10 years ago. Little did I know, that those words would end up leading me to write a book based on that song. I was living in Tennessee at the time, and had met a very talented young songwriter a few months before that fateful day. He happened to be standing outside the music publishing company that he was signed with. I was driving around music row, which if you don't already know, it's the place in Nashville, where practically all the hit songs get written and recorded, and all the business deals happen in the country music industry. I had stopped to ask for directions to another place I was going on Music Row. I saw this young outlaw/rock star looking guy, walking in the back-alley parking lot of a music publishing company. So, I asked him if he knew how to get where I needed to go. We got to talking music, so we shared with each other what we had going on musically. That's what happens on Music Row. Networking is everything when you're trying to get your music into the right hands, or trying to get any kind of music deal done. He was extremely friendly, so I said, "we should write some time," because he seemed genuinely interested in the project my family and I were working on. So, I got his phone number, and ended up booking a songwriting session with him.

When you book a songwriting session with someone, it's basically a team effort to write the best song possible ... kind of like a songwriting master mind. One of the most important things is that you don't show up to the session without ideas for a great song. Otherwise, if you just show up, and the other person has the great idea along with the music, you end up basically getting credit for a song you didn't have a whole lot of help or input into writing. Which means the songwriter or songwriters won't want to write with you in the future, and word will most likely get around the Music Row songwriting community that you're not a very good person to co-write with. Which means that you're not going to have a whole lot of success, because just about every hit song in Nashville has been written by at least 2 people. So, for this particular songwriting session, I wanted to come up with something great because my friend was a signed songwriter with a great publishing company, and I wasn't a signed songwriter. Very rarely do signed songwriters want to write with an unsigned songwriter, or unsigned band, because the big marketing and promotion money, won't be spent on the musical project or song. If you're not familiar with what it means to be a signed songwriter, it's pretty much the same thing as having a record deal, except that the company pays you an advance each month for you to write songs, instead of going out and singing songs. So basically, you're the guy or girl who most people don't know, but you're extremely important, because without a great song you have nothing. The greatest singer in the world could sing a lame song and it wouldn't matter how good the singer was because a bad song is a bad song.

My friend and I ended up putting our songwriting session on the calendar a few days after meeting on that fateful day. I knew I had to bring a song idea to the session, that was different and outstanding, in- order for the opportunity to write another song, in the future, with my talented new friend. I didn't want to blow it, because he had Sony Records looking to sign him to a record deal, and timing is everything when you're networking with up and coming writers or artists. So, I came up with an idea from out of nowhere. When that happens, it's like it's being downloaded from the heavenly iCloud into my brain. I started hearing this melody for a chorus. So, I picked up my guitar and started playing it. Now the music starts speaking to me, and it then translates into words. So, the next day, I showed up to my writing appointment, and I see my friend at the office, and he doesn't look very good; meaning, I could tell that something was wrong. So, I asked my friend, "What's going on?" He then begins to tell me something that has always been my biggest nightmare. He said that a few days ago, he felt a lump in his arm pit, and decided to go to the doctor to have it checked out. It was a tumor, so the doctor did a biopsy on it. As my friend and I were speaking, he was literally waiting on a call from the doctor's office as to whether the tumor was malignant or benign, which is just a fancy doctor's term to describe whether it's cancerous or not. For that kind of news, the doctor doesn't just tell you over the phone if it is or isn't cancer. So, the call would come in and then he would have to drive to the doctor's office in person to find out his fate. I told my friend how sorry I was to hear about his situation, and that if he wanted to cancel our writing appointment, that I would, of course, understand. He told me that something told him to go through with the appointment, and that it's better to keep his mind off the call he was waiting for.

I told my friend that I was glad he wanted to still write because I believed I had the perfect song to write under these circumstances. I began to tell him that the song is about life as it relates to football. How life is all about getting the next first down, to keep the drive-in life alive. That by the inch it's a cinch, but by the yard it's hard. I also told him that the line I really felt strong about was, "It *ain't* ever over at Half Time," and that's where the magic began. In Nashville, the songwriting community is pretty small. There's only so many signed writers, and your reputation follows you close. You need to make sure that you have the right rapport with whoever you're writing with. I knew that my friend could use some prayer with what he was going through. So, I asked him if he would mind if I prayed for him and for the song we were about to write and finish. He said that he would really appreciate it if we could pray together. So. I prayed one of the most heartfelt prayers that I had ever prayed in my life. It was about helping my friend to get through this time of fear, and that God would pull him through this, even if it was Cancer. I prayed that he would be healed either way, and that he would be an inspiration to others no matter what happened. I also prayed for God to give us the words and the music, to finish the song, that would be called "Halftime."

After our prayer, we started writing the song, or I might even say, that the song started writing itself. It took about an hour, and the song was finished. The song ended up being about the title of this book. It was a song that I would consider to be a therapeutic song that anyone could listen to, and feel like they just went through a 3-minute motivational music seminar. I usually don't feel that way about songs that I write, but this one, in particular, did not seem like one I wrote, but one that someone else wrote who simply inspired and encouraged me. The song is about living your life like a football player ... playing out the 2-minute warning at the end of the 4th quarter in a football game. It can also be applied to any sport, where there's just a couple of minutes left on the clock, and the person who we rely on for the plan to win the game of life. No great team has ever been without a great coach, and in life, we all have someone who we look up to or get advice from. You can hear the song we wrote that day by clicking this link.

http://DarrenTaylorMusic.com

Let Me Introduce You to My Coach

DISCLAIMER ....

I want to make sure that you, or anyone else who reads this book, understands, that I'm not claiming to be perfect. I'm a self-professed sinner, who tries to rely on my "Life Coach" to overcome any problems or sins that I struggle with in life. I used to wear a mask, and tried to make it look like I was perfect. Fortunately, I had the right Coach in my life who led me to understand how important it was to take off the mask of being fake, and to be real with others and myself. I'm not trying to judge anyone who may still be wearing a mask to try and fool everyone into thinking that they are perfect and never have any problems. I'm simply trying to introduce them to "The Greatest Coach of All Time" who's teachings have helped me to take my mask off, and to help others do the same. I'm one beggar wanting to show my fellow beggars, where the food is. The following story, is told by my life Coach. In this story, He is describing the types of people He is willing to coach. The types of people He wants on His team.

Luke 18:9-14

> [9] *To some who were confident of their own righteousness and looked down on everyone else, Jesus told this parable:* [10] *"Two men went up to the temple to pray, one a Pharisee and the other a tax collector.* [11] *The Pharisee stood by himself*

and prayed: 'God, I thank you that I am not like other people—robbers, evildoers, adulterers—or even like this tax collector. ¹²I fast twice a week and give a tenth of all I get.'

¹³"But the tax collector stood at a distance. He would not even look up to heaven, but beat his breast and said, 'God, have mercy on me, a sinner.'

¹⁴"I tell you that this man, rather than the other, went home justified before God. For all those who exalt themselves will be humbled, and those who humble themselves will be exalted."

HE WANTS TO HELP YOU TO LIVE YOUR DREAMS

John 10:10 - *The thief comes only to steal and kill and destroy; I have come that they may have life, and have it to the full.*

Some of the people, we look to for advice, may be coming from a good place and some of them give us advice from a bad place but, either way, we all get advice from somewhere and someone. So, I believe, that in life, we all need a coach. If you've ever played on an organized sports team, you know exactly what I'm talking about. Without the coach to help us get into the right physical condition, and the right mental condition, we most likely won't be able to win. We need someone who can help us have the right plays and game plan. Someone to inspire and encourage us, to be our best. Someone who will tell us the truth out of love and who won't pull any punches. And that's what the song "Halftime" is all about. That's what this book is all about. It's about "The Greatest Coach of All Time & His Game Changing Play Book for Your Comeback." My prayer for you is that this book makes you realize, that no matter what you're going through in your life, no matter how defeated you feel at this present moment, you can get to know "The Greatest Coach of All Time," as not just your Coach, but also your personal Lord and Savior.

Even if your own father or mother never showed up to watch your games when you were growing up, this Coach has always been there, watching all your games. He's always been cheering for you in your own personal game of life that He customized just for you. He rigged the game in your favor, and guarantees victory for you IF you're willing to let Him coach you. No matter how bad things are in your life right now, and no matter how badly you believe that you're losing in life, it's not too late for a come from behind victory. It's time for your comeback. You can, and you will come back!!! You're reading this book for a reason. This is meant to be. So, with no further ado, let's get to know this Coach better than you ever have or thought you could. Let's get ready to celebrate your victorious comeback!!

Who Is the Greatest Coach of All Time?

You could ask people all over the world who they think the best coach of all time is, and many of them would give you a name that you or I have never heard of. Especially, if it's a team from a different country and for a sport that you're not a big fan of. But who do you think is the greatest coach of all time? It doesn't have to be someone who's the coach of a professional team. It could be someone who was your little league baseball coach. Or maybe it was your Junior high basketball coach. If you're a fan of pro football, then perhaps you watched Super Bowl LI, between the New England Patriots, and the Atlanta Falcons. Even if you're not a football fan, there's no way you could have watched that game, and not been converted into one. I have never watched any sporting event, and been so convinced, that one team would lose, more than I was in that game. The Patriots were getting humiliated on the field. Tom Brady had an axe to grind because of his previous deflate gate suspension, and it didn't look like he would get his revenge. You can go online and see a video of what I believe to be the greatest comeback victory of all time for a football team. But the greatest comeback of all time, will be revealed to you later in this book. So, keep reading, or you're going to be kept in the dark, wondering who I'm talking about. Deal?

Getting back to the Patriots. While you're watching, make sure you look for that one-play that would be considered the game changer. The moment where all the momentum shifted, and the feeling of whoever was watching, went from there's no way the Patriots could win this, to the Patriots just may win this. After all, the Patriots do have a couple of people in their organization who some may say the greatest coach of all time is Bill Belichik, along with Tom Brady, who is considered, by many, to be the greatest quarterback of all time. But the bottom line is that this game looked like it was completely over. Which brings me to who I believe is the greatest Player/Coach of all time.

He was in the game called Life, and ended up having the greatest comeback of all time. His comeback was the game changer for your life, my life, and anyone else who would come before or after Him. His road to victory looked like all hope of winning was completely dead ... literally dead. He was whipped, beaten, mocked, spit on and crucified, by the opposing team, who I'm going to refer to as, "The Hell City Demons." And finally, just before He took his last breath on the cross, He said, *"It is finished."* So, what exactly was He saying was finished? Was He finished? Because after all, He was about to take his last breath. Blood was dripping from His body and onto the cross, as the nails had pierced His wrists and His feet. The crown of long thorns was dripping blood, because they were lodged deeply into His head. So. what exactly was finished? I don't want to assume that you know who I'm talking about, because perhaps you may be reading this book in a translated language, and "The Greatest Coach of All Time" hasn't been revealed to you yet. But my guess would be, that you know exactly who I'm talking about. So most likely, you guessed it. I'm talking about Jesus Christ, the Son of God, the King of Kings. That carpenter guy who was born a long time ago, from a mother, who was still a virgin at the time of giving birth to her Son.

Maybe you're an atheist, who doesn't believe in Jesus Christ even being real. Or maybe you do believe in Jesus, but think He was just a man, and His comeback victory over death was a made-up fraud. Either way, I encourage you to keep reading this book, because my hope in writing this book, is that Jesus Christ becomes the personal Lord and Savior over your life, and that you look to Him as your personal Coach, who can coach you to your amazing come from behind victory in your life.

And that victory, is to finish the game of life strong, and that your victory leads your friends and family to victory as well. So, what exactly was the victory of Jesus? I believe quite plainly, that His victory, was the victory over death, as well as victory over evil. He could have been one of two things, the victim or victor. Fortunately for you and me, he became the victor. Though I'm not an expert on the Bible, I have been reading it just about every day, for the last 20 years. The times I wasn't reading the Bible, I found that I wasn't doing as good as I could have been doing. I'm here to tell you, that you don't need to be a church preacher, or an author, to read what I'm going to refer to in this book as "His Playbook" or "The Bible." So, let's get started, in discussing, why I believe Jesus is, and always will be, "The Greatest Coach of All Time" and why you should trust Him to be the Coach over your life.

HE CREATED THE GAME AND HAS EQUIPPED YOU TO WIN

2 Peter 1:20-21

> [20] *Above all, you must understand that no prophecy of Scripture came about by the prophet's own interpretation of things.* [21] *For prophecy never had its origin in the human will, but prophets, though human, spoke from God as they were carried along by the Holy Spirit.*

2 Timothy 3:16-17

> [16] *All Scripture is God-breathed and is useful for teaching, rebuking, correcting and training in righteousness,* [17] *so that the servant of God may be thoroughly equipped for every good work.*

John 1:1-2

> [1] *In the beginning was the Word, and the Word was with God, and the Word was God.* [2] *He was with God in the beginning.*

I believe that the Bible is the incorruptible Word of God. I believe that it's the owner's manual for us humans. If you believe what I believe, from the scripture above, then you believe that not only did God make us humans, but that He made everything that has ever been made. That includes things that are seen and unseen. Just to make sure that you're not confused with who the Word is, and who God is, let me tell you how I understand it. In John 1:1-2, the scripture says, that *"The 'Word' was with God, and The Word was God."* He was with God in the beginning. Huh? Sounds a bit confusing to most people including myself when I first read it. I believe that Jesus is The Word, and when He says throughout the Bible, that He and The Father are one, He really means it. If you have a cup of water, then you can have two more forms of that water. You can have that water become steam, and you can also have that water become ice cubes. Either way, it's still water but just in a different form.

If you're semi familiar with Christianity, then you may have heard of the Trinity. The Trinity is God the Father, God the Son, and God the Holy Spirit. All are God, but in different forms, for His different purposes. But the bottom-line is that much of what God does, is not always figured out by us humans. So, what I want to discuss with you is why we should trust Jesus Christ to be our Coach, and why I believe that He's not just our personal Lord and Savior, but that He can, and should also be considered, our Life Coach. If you're into video games, then you may understand what I'm about to say. If someone created a video game, and did all the coding, and knows everything there is to know about the game, including the outcome and shortcuts to victory, wouldn't you want that person to tell you what to do in the game regarding winning? Of course, you would. So, if Jesus was, and still is, The Word, and if He's one with God, and created everything that is seen and unseen, then why wouldn't we want to read His manual/playbook to coach us to our comeback? In His book, are written, many of the rules of the game and many of the plays to victory. You'll have to read the Bible for yourself to get all of them.

If you were about to take a history test in class, and you knew you could have the history book with you at your desk, while you're taking the test, to make sure you pass with an A+, wouldn't that be something you would want to do? Sadly enough, the enemy known as, "The Hell City Demons," have tricked every one of their opponents into thinking that we don't need to know the rules to play by, and we don't need to know the creator of the game. You see, "The Hell City Demons" already know that they lose the game. The only thing they know they can do, is to take as many of their opponents on "Team Jesus," back to Hell City with them, when the game is over. After all, "The Hell City Demons" have a rally cry. It's "Let's Give 'em' Hell." That's exactly what the Bible says the losers in this game of life will receive. The reason you and I don't need to worry, is that we have a Coach who guarantees us victory. And that's why, throughout your life, you may have been asked by someone or some program, if you know the truth. The truth is that you don't have to lose. As a matter-of-fact, you get to win simply by choosing to be on the winning team and being coached by the winningest Coach of all time, who happens to be undefeated. He's coached billions of people to victory throughout the beginning of man and woman kind. The good news is that wherever you find yourself in the game of life, as-long-as there's still a breath in you, you can still win by choosing to be on "Team Jesus," because victory is guaranteed with "Team Jesus." Defeat is guaranteed, if you choose to be on "The Hell City Demons."

The following bible verse tells us what we need to do to be on "Team Jesus."

John 3:16 For God so loved the world that he gave his one and only Son, that whoever believes in him shall not perish but have eternal life.

Jesus is a coach who literally died for us to be on His team! Our Coach is also the Savior of the world. We get to be on His team for all eternity. Have you joined His team yet?

Whether you know it or not, you may be playing on "The Hell City Demons" team without even realizing it. In Luke 11:23, Jesus says the following, *[23]"Whoever is not with me is against me, and whoever does not gather with me scatters."*

Please do some soul searching, right now, and ask yourself, whose team are you playing on? If you're on the wrong team, it's not too late to switch teams, as-long-as you're still alive. In the next chapter, I'm going to discuss a guy who found that to be true, straight from Jesus' mouth.

The Greatest "Last Minute" Comeback Ever "The Thief on The Cross"

Luke 23:39-43

> ³⁹One of the criminals who hung there, hurled insults at him: "Aren't you the Messiah? Save yourself and us!"
>
> ⁴⁰But the other criminal rebuked him. "Don't you fear God," he said, "since you are under the same sentence? ⁴¹We are punished justly, for we are getting what our deeds deserve. But this man has done nothing wrong."
>
> ⁴²Then he said, "Jesus, remember me when you come into your kingdom."
>
> ⁴³Jesus answered him, "Truly I tell you, today you will be with me in paradise."

Wow!!! I just realized how much I have never fully appreciated the game changing moment in the life of the thief hanging on the cross next to Jesus. It's clear to me that this thief who defended Jesus against the attacks of the other thief on the cross, was told that he would be with Jesus in Paradise that very same day. The thief on the cross who defended Jesus and, also, confessed and acknowledged his sin, saying that he, himself, deserved the punishment of death on a cross, was all

Jesus needed from the thief, to bring him to Paradise that very same day. But notice how the thief had to acknowledge to Jesus the fact that he was a sinner and asked Jesus to remember him when he gets to His kingdom. Basically, he was asking Jesus if he could be on His team. He switched over from the "Hell City Demons" to "Team Jesus." And that's what's so amazing about this true story. Jesus knew this guy's heart, and that was enough for him to make the Team. There's no mention of how good the thief on the cross could throw. There's no mention of how fast he could run. The tryout for "Team Jesus" consisted of the thief on the cross simply believing in Jesus to lead him to the winner's circle. Jesus already won the game by defeating "The Hell City Demons" and death, by dying on the cross, and coming back to life after 3 days.

We just discussed Jesus dying on the cross and then being raised from the dead after 3 days BUT, did you hear about Lazarus who was a personal, friend of Jesus? Jesus raised Lazarus from the dead after being dead for 4 days? The thief on the cross was perhaps minutes away from dying. It sounds like this guy was a life-long criminal who was literally in the 2-minute warning of his life but was still able to win. He won by watching and learning from Jesus on the cross and by listening to what Jesus said. Jesus was still reaching out to the lost even while He was going through the punishment He did not deserve. For example, ... in Luke 23:34 Jesus said, *"Father forgive them for they know not what they are doing."* That was forgiveness, right there on the cross, while Jesus was being wrongly accused and punished to death. The thief on the cross heard what Jesus said and believed that Jesus was the Savior from what he saw and heard. Now keep in mind that the saved thief on the cross had most likely heard what people were saying about Jesus Christ before hanging next to Him. After all, Jesus had been in His ministry for over 2 years healing the sick and giving sight back to the blind. While Jesus was doing all of this, the saved thief on the cross was doing his own thing. So, the point is that the saved thief on the cross decided to trust the One he had heard was the Savior of the world, the Messiah that was to come into the world and save Israel ... not just Israel but the whole world and that's the choice anyone who's alive in this world today has.

If they hear about Jesus and don't decide as to what they believe, now is the time ... we only have this moment. Not to sound morbid or discouraging, but you don't know how much time you have left to make your decision of which team you're going to play on. I'll cover that in the next chapter.

Life Can Be Here Today and Gone Today

> James 4:14: *"Why, you do not even know what will happen tomorrow. What is your life? You are a mist that appears for a little while and then vanishes."*

That is perhaps the most sobering Scripture in the entire Bible that I don't think anyone can disagree with. Yet most of us procrastinate when going for our dreams, because we have convinced ourselves that we're guaranteed to live to be at least 100 years old. A few years back, I was thinking about how we are all going to die, and that we'll all unfortunately have to go through a most likely painful physical death, because that's the way it is. But, there is an exception to the rule. That exception is only if Jesus comes back to gather up his saved people before we go through our physical death. The bottom-line is that I don't think you or I should hold our breath for that circumstance. So, I thought particularly about all the people who were living in Abraham Lincoln's day and age. Abraham Lincoln died on April 15th, 1865, which was 152 years ago. I realized that every single person who was living on the face of planet earth at that time, had to go through a physical death. So, here's my point ... It's time to decide as to which team, and which coach, you want to play for. Do you want to play for the "Heaven City Angels," or do you want to play for the "Hell City Demons"? It's important to make that decision before it's too late. In the next chapter, we'll discuss what Jesus is able to do for his friends.

Jesus Brought Lazarus Back to Life After Being Dead For 4 Days

The Death of Lazarus

John 11:1-4

¹Now a man named Lazarus was sick. He was from Bethany, the village of Mary and her sister Martha. ²(This Mary, whose brother Lazarus now lay sick, was the same one who poured perfume on the Lord and wiped his feet with her hair.) ³So the sisters sent word to Jesus, "Lord, the one you love is sick."

⁴When he heard this, Jesus said, "This sickness will not end in death. No, it is for God's glory so that God's Son may be glorified through it." ⁵Now Jesus loved Martha and her sister and Lazarus. ⁶So when he heard that Lazarus was sick, he stayed where he was two more days, ⁷and then he said to his disciples, "Let us go back to Judea."

⁸"But Rabbi," they said, "a short while ago the Jews there tried to stone you, and yet you are going back?"

⁹Jesus answered, "Are there not twelve hours of daylight? Anyone who walks in the daytime will not stumble, for they see by this world's light. ¹⁰It is when a person walks at night that they stumble, for they have no light."

¹¹After he had said this, he went on to tell them, "Our friend Lazarus has fallen asleep, but I am going there to wake him up."

¹²His disciples replied, "Lord, if he sleeps, he will get better." ¹³Jesus had been speaking of his death, but his disciples thought he meant natural sleep.

¹⁴So then he told them plainly, "Lazarus is dead, ¹⁵and for your sake I am glad I was not there, so that you may believe. But let us go to him."

¹⁶Then Thomas (also known as Didymus*) said to the rest of the disciples, "Let us also go, that we may die with him."

Jesus Comforts the Sisters of Lazarus

¹⁷On his arrival, Jesus found that Lazarus had already been in the tomb for four days. ¹⁸Now Bethany was less than two miles from Jerusalem, ¹⁹and many Jews had come to Martha and Mary to comfort them in the loss of their brother. ²⁰When Martha heard that Jesus was coming, she went out to meet him, but Mary stayed at home.

²¹"Lord," Martha said to Jesus, "if you had been here, my brother would not have died. ²²But I know that even now God will give you whatever you ask."

²³Jesus said to her, "Your brother will rise again."

²⁴Martha answered, "I know he will rise again in the resurrection at the last day."

²⁵ Jesus said to her, "I am the resurrection and the life. The one who believes in me will live, even though they die; ²⁶ and whoever lives by believing in me will never die. Do you believe this?"

²⁷ "Yes, Lord," she replied, "I believe that you are the Messiah, the Son of God, who is to come into the world."

²⁸ After she had said this, she went back and called her sister Mary aside. "The Teacher is here," she said, "and is asking for you." ²⁹ When Mary heard this, she got up quickly and went to him. ³⁰ Now Jesus had not yet entered the village, but was still at the place where Martha had met him. ³¹ When the Jews who had been with Mary in the house, comforting her, noticed how quickly she got up and went out, they followed her, supposing she was going to the tomb to mourn there.

³² When Mary reached the place where Jesus was and saw him, she fell at his feet and said, "Lord, if you had been here, my brother would not have died."

³³ When Jesus saw her weeping, and the Jews who had come along with her also weeping, he was deeply moved in spirit and troubled. ³⁴ "Where have you laid him?" he asked.

"Come and see, Lord," they replied.

³⁵ Jesus wept.

³⁶ Then the Jews said, "See how He loved him!"

³⁷ But some of them said, "Could not He who opened the eyes of the blind man have kept this man from dying?"

Jesus Raises Lazarus From the Dead

³⁸Jesus, once more deeply moved, came to the tomb. It was a cave with a stone laid across the entrance. ³⁹"Take away the stone," He said.

"But, Lord," said Martha, the sister of the dead man, "by this time there is a bad odor, for he has been there four days."

⁴⁰Then Jesus said, "Did I not tell you that if you believe, you will see the glory of God?"

⁴¹So they took away the stone. Then Jesus looked up and said, "Father, I thank you that you have heard me. ⁴²I knew that you always hear me, but I said this for the benefit of the people standing here, that they may believe that you sent me."

⁴³When he had said this, Jesus called in a loud voice, "Lazarus come out!" The dead man came out, his hands and feet wrapped with strips of linen, and a cloth around his face.

Jesus said to them, "Take off the grave clothes and let him go."

I don't know about you, but I think that's an incredible story. But what's even more incredible, is that it's true! Do you agree with me? If not, that's ok. Keep reading, and I'll see if I can help you to believe!

Rudy!!! Rudy!!! You're More Than Just a Ruettiger!!!

If you're into sports movies like I am, then perhaps you've seen the movie, "Rudy." It's perhaps the greatest true sports story in college football history. So, if you've already seen it, I'll tell you my take on the moral of the story, and how it relates to the kind of players Jesus is looking for. Rudy Ruettiger is a guy who's all heart. He isn't very big, and he doesn't look like the kind of guy who would make Notre Dame's football team. His dream was to play football for Notre Dame, but in-order-to even have the chance to try out, he had to get accepted into Notre Dame. He had every reason to give up, and every person in his life telling him to just give up the dream, and settle into mediocrity. Even his Dad said to him, "You're a Ruettiger, and playing football for Notre Dame and achieving your dreams isn't for Ruettigers." His Dad told him to just give up, and to be grateful and happy, about settling for less in his life. In the movie, his father and brother both worked for the same company in a dangerous mediocre job. I won't ruin the whole movie for you if you didn't see it. But I will tell you that he ends up going against his earthly father's advice and following the advice of his Heavenly Father. Rudy ends up making the team as a walk-on, and becomes an inspirational college football legend!! Feeling discouraged today? Watch "Rudy" today. By the end of the movie, you'll have the wind back in your sails.

I don't know about you and the relationship you had with your father, but my dad was a great man who tried his absolute best to raise me right. He was a single father of me and my two brothers at the age of 37. He struggled his whole adult life with a severe alcohol and prescription medication addiction problem. The reason I call it an alcohol and prescription medication addiction problem, is because I don't believe that somebody is an alcoholic or a drug addict. It's not who they are, it's just an addiction that they have, that can be overcome. The reason I bring up my dad's personal struggle with his addictions, is because he was very open about it and would have wanted the story of his struggles to help others to overcome their own struggles as well. His dream was to be a pitcher in the major leagues. He was born and raised in Chicago, Illinois, and he was an amazing pitcher, with one heck of a wicked curveball, changeup, and fastball. When I was growing up he would play catch with me, and would only give me a tiny taste of his fastball. It was fast enough to break your hand. My dad taught me to play baseball, but his birth father wasn't there to teach him how to play. He grew up with an abusive father who also had an addiction to alcohol. Unfortunately, my dad wasn't supported by his birth father to pursue his dream of baseball. But luckily his stepfather came along, and was incredibly supportive of my dad and his dream.

Something very tragic had happened in my dad's life during the time he was pitching for a farm league team in Chicago, which was a stepping stone to pitching for the Chicago White Sox. My dad had gotten a job with an elevator company that was part of the union in Chicago. It was a family thing and It paid very well, and it was what my dad decided to do. His job was to fix the elevators at the buildings in Chicago. Quite a few of them were well over 20 stories high. One day while he was still young, and pursuing his dream of playing baseball in the big leagues, he was working at a job to fix an elevator, and while being in the elevator shaft, where the elevator would go up and down through the building, he fell three floors down, in between the elevator shaft, and was severely cut open, and it crushed his shoulder of his pitching arm, as well as the side of his stomach. He was bleeding to death, and it didn't look like he was going to live, but his elevator partner called for help, and the paramedics brought him to the hospital, which saved his life. He was in the hospital recovering for around 6 months. It was very bad. He had more stitches in his body than a baseball, and he was on pain killers, due to the massive pain he had to endure. When he finally got out of the hospital, and it was time to try and pitch again, his throwing arm wasn't the same as it had been before. So, he began to drink, and take pain killers over the mourning of the loss of his dream.

The reason I wanted to share my dad's story with you, is because he had a dream, and it didn't happen. So, when it came to his own sons' dreams, he was jaded and he no longer believed in dreams happening for himself or us. To him it meant that you shouldn't pursue your dreams, because in the end, they only end in disappointment and pain. And what loving father doesn't want to spare his children pain and disappointment? However, his disappointment and pain carried over to me and my brothers. I personally had the dream of being a famous singer for as long as I can remember. But as I grew older, my Dad made it clear to me that I should just oddly enough join the elevator union and forsake my dream for a steady paycheck. He would constantly tell me that the odds of making it in the music business was like winning the lottery. It was very discouraging to hear him say that on a regular basis, but I went for my dream regardless. Even though my dad lost his dream to working and almost dying in the elevator repair industry, he had stayed in that industry once his dream of playing in the big leagues was lost. So, what does this story of Rudy Ruettiger, and his negative dad, have to do with you or me? It has everything to do with you and me because, in-spite-of what our earthly fathers may believe and feel about making our dreams come true, we have a Heavenly Father, who says that He believes in us, and supports all our righteous dreams coming true. He helps us to make our dreams become a reality. And when we feel like giving up, He gives us strength to keep going.

Philippians 4:*13:*" *I can do ALL things though Him who gives me strength."*

ALL things mean ALL things. Not just some things. Jesus says we should go for ALL our dreams and the victory will be ours. That's why

He's "The Greatest Coach of All Time." He not only says we will win with his guidance, but He also gives us the strength we need and His belief in us to keep going, until we achieve our dreams. What dream have you given up on? It's time to resurrect it!!

Some of the All-Star Players Jesus Has Coached

Love him or hate him, Tim Tebow has had a miraculous career. And although Tim has had many earthly coaches, he makes it no secret who His Coach really is. After every victory, he thanks Jesus Christ. Many people say that Jesus doesn't take an interest in who wins football games. But if you look at a football game as a way for people to be inspired by what they watch out on the football field, then I believe it's another way for us to not only be entertained, but encouraged to persevere or push through whatever obstacles we face in our own lives. The early story of Tim Tebow, is that his mother was told that she should abort Tim in the womb, because the Doctor performed a test and said Tim would be born with special needs. But his mother and father decided to trust God that the baby would be fine, even if that was the case. So, they decided to let Tim be born.

Tim has had many haters throughout his life and career, but I think he has a lot of fans as well. I'm one of them. When I watched Tim play as the starting quarterback for the Denver Broncos in the playoffs, some of the things that transpired out on the field were miraculous. But what was even more astonishing, is that during one of the miraculous come from behind victories, there was a halo above mile high stadium, during and after the come from behind victory was complete. You can just google "Halo above football stadium Tim Tebow", and see what I'm talking about. It was awesome!! Coincidence? I don't' think so. But it seemed to me like a sign from God, that He cared about that game.

Tim was talking about Jesus to the press all the time, and he would get down on bended knee with many of the other players the moment each game ended. It was really inspiring to watch as a Christian. I couldn't help thinking that God was with Tim during his games, because He was willing to give Jesus the glory, honor and the credit for his blessings and victories.

I think God gave the halo above the stadium as a sign to encourage His people, and to let them know that He had a personal hand in that victory. Some would ask, "Well why would God favor one quarterback over the other, or one team over the other?" My question to you is, "Which quarterback was publicly giving all honor and praise to Jesus for the victory?" God chooses His leaders, and is very pleased when they give Him the credit He is due for His role in the victory. And one of His roles is, "The Coach." After the door closed on Tim Tebow's career in football, he was given the opportunity to play in the minor leagues for the New York Mets minor league baseball team. I just saw on the news last week, that in Tim's very first at bat in the minor leagues for the Mets, he hit a home run. I'm sure there will be many more home runs for Tim, because he publicly acknowledges who his Coach really is. The Good News is that Jesus wants to be your "Life Coach" as well. The Scripture below made me understand how Jesus will feel about us if we're embarrassed, or ashamed to tell people about Him and His Words.

Are you ashamed to tell people about Jesus?

> Mark 8:38: 38 *"If anyone is ashamed of me and my words in this adulterous and sinful generation, the Son of Man will be ashamed of them when he comes in his Father's glory with the holy angels."*

His Star Quarterback

We just discussed one of the players He is coaching in today's modern time. Now let's get into some of the players Jesus coached over 2 thousand years ago. Players who you may, or may not have heard of. One of them was a guitar playing shepherd of sheep, who was the youngest of many brothers. He happened to be very good at using a sling and a stone as a weapon against lions, bears, and many other wild animals, who would threaten the flock of sheep under his care. His name is David. He was referred to by God in the Bible as "The Apple of His Eye." Throughout his life, he was involved in some major sin, but God still referred to Him as "The Apple of His Eye." And that's because David was all heart. He's the guy who went from being a young shepherd boy to a king. Perhaps you heard of the victory that he had over a real-life giant named Goliath.

I think you've most likely heard the story, but do you really believe it to be true, or do you think it's a made-up story? Either way, I'd like to dissect how that victory was won. David was an athlete. Instead of being a quarterback who threw passes, he threw stones with a sling. And he always hit the receiver. He was so good at it, he killed the giant with one stone. He trained in the field with just his sheep, but finally stepped into the game when his time had come in front of King Saul, along with many of Israel's soldiers, of which his older brothers were a part of. They all doubted him. The armor they wanted him to wear, didn't fit ... it was too big! Everyone said he couldn't do it, and that he would die. They said he didn't have what it takes. They were ALL wrong! David knew who his

Coach was. And he knew the many previous victories that he had won over the lions, bears and other enemies who tried to attack his flock. So, this time was no different than the others. The only difference is that David finally had an audience to witness the victory. But what was so important, is that David gave the credit for the victory to his Coach.

1 Samuel 17:46

> David says ... *"This day the Lord will deliver you into my hands, and I'll strike you down and cut off your head. This very day I will give the carcasses of the Philistine army to the birds and the wild animals, and the whole world will know that there is a God in Israel."*

I don't know about you, but it sure sounds like David took no credit whatsoever for that victory. He simply states that, *"This day the Lord will deliver you into my hands, and I'll strike you down and cut off your head."* Wow!!! Talk about confidence. Cutting off Goliath's head was a hardcore victory, and it was a victory to be told throughout the ages. It's a testimony as to who gives us the victory. It reminds me of a movie called, "Facing the Giants." If you haven't seen it, you should, definitely, see it right away. You won't see anyone's head getting cut off, but you will, definitely, be inspired to go for your dreams, knowing that Jesus is there, beside you, coaching you to victory. Getting back to David. If you haven't read what I like to refer to as "His Game Changing Playbook," otherwise known as the Bible, I highly recommend you read it to hear the rest of the true story of David, who would later become King David. The story of a young shepherd boy, who was a sinner just like you and me, but became one of the greatest victors of all time.

There are so many stories in the Bible about men and women who were weak in the current condition they were in, when Jesus called them to play on His team. But they became star players for "The Heaven City Angels." It has been said, that when the student is ready, the teacher will appear. Are you ready? Are you sick and tired of feeling and being defeated? Are you tired of being discouraged and depressed, because you're playing on the losing team? Are you ready to start celebrating victory after victory? If so, keep reading, because you're closer to your comeback than you think.

Jesus' Players Become Talent Scouts for His Team

Mark 1:16-18

> *[16] As Jesus walked beside the Sea of Galilee, He saw Simon and his brother Andrew casting a net into the lake, for they were fishermen. [17] "Come, follow Me," Jesus said, "and I will send you out to fish for people." [18] At once they left their nets and followed Him.*

That Scripture clearly shows how Jesus is wanting to recruit, and have us recruit as many people as we can for His team. In fact, He has an unlimited number of spots on His roster. If you're not familiar with the word "disciple," it means "a student of." Jesus tells His would be disciples/players what He wants them to do. When He says that He will send them out to fish for people, He is saying that He wants us to go out and recruit people to be on His Team. All great teams, whether in business or sports, have recruiters or talent scouts. I don't know if you've ever fished before, but if not, I'll explain the process to you. When I was growing up, my dad would take us fishing all the time. We had a summer home in Wisconsin, and we had a couple of ponds on our property. My Dad paid for it to be stocked with lots of bass. We pretty much would catch a fish every time we would cast out by either using bait or using a lure. I loved fishing in our ponds because I knew I would catch lots of fish.

Matthew 9:37 *Then He said to his disciples. "The harvest is plentiful but the workers are few."*

That Scripture describes what it was like to fish in the two ponds that my dad had stocked full of fish. The people that fished in those ponds were just me, my brothers, and my dad. Sometimes, people would sneak on to our property to fish in the ponds when we would leave town to go back to our home in Illinois. One time my brother and I, along with a few friends of ours, drove up to Wisconsin for the first time on our own without our dad, because my brother had just gotten his driver's license. It was a crazy trip. When we showed up to the summer home, there was this pot smoking *hippie* guy smoking weed and fishing from our pier. We came up to him and asked him if he knew the owner of the property. He said "No," and we then told him that you're looking at the owners. He looked at us with doubt because we were 16-year old kids. Plus, he was really stoned, and kind of freaking out a bit. He also seemed a bit stressed out because he didn't expect to get "busted" fishing on our property. We decided to let him stay and fish, because he was honest with us about not knowing the owner of the property.

So how does this story relate to Jesus saying that He'll send us out to fish for people? And what does Jesus mean when He says that "the harvest is plentiful but the workers are few?" I think it says that He needs more fisherman, because the world is stocked with people who we need to catch to be on "Team Jesus." He wants us to recruit them to be on His team, so they can live a happy and victorious life, and so they can stop losing, and being miserable in life. But most importantly, He wants them to spend eternity with Him in Heaven, after they have transitioned from their physical body to their Spiritual body. He doesn't take His Players to Disney World, He takes them to Heaven!

THE BENEFITS OF BEING COACHED BY JESUS

So, what are the benefits of being coached by "The Greatest Coach of All Time?" There are so many life changing benefits, so let's get into it! The number one benefit is that you will no longer have a constant feeling of emptiness, that accompanies a life of defeat, in a meaningless game, where victory can never be achieved. You'll be like a dog who no longer chases it's tail in vain, like us humans who can chase victory in vain. On the opposing team, there is no real victory. There is only a lie. A lie that tells you that competing against "The One" Who created you and the game, will give you happiness and satisfaction. That couldn't be farther from the truth. I can personally tell you that I used to try to be happy by feasting daily at the buffet of sin. I tried to fill the void in my life with food, sex, drugs, women and rock and roll. I tried to fill it with money ... none of it worked. The coach of the opposing team has many names. But for right now, let's just call him "The Liar." It's such a fitting name for him, because the Bible says that he is the father of lies, and that lying is his native tongue.

> John 8:44: Jesus says, *"You belong to your father, the devil, and you want to carry out your father's desires. He was a murderer from the beginning, not holding to the truth, for there is no truth in him. When he lies, he speaks his native language, for he is a liar and the father of lies."*

Now that you know what Jesus says about the coach of the other team. Why on God's green earth would you ever want to play for a coach like that? Make no mistake about it … the devil is the coach of the opposing team. Instead of happiness and peace, his players receive pain and death. They receive broken marriages, broken relationships with their kids, and a web of lies and deceit that they could never become free of, unless they were to switch teams and play on "Team Jesus." Unfortunately, the end prize for those on "Team Satan," is an eternal separation from Jesus, and a permanent residence in hell, along with all your teammates and coach. I've often thought about why anyone would be sent to hell, and away from Jesus, as the punishment for choosing to be on the opposing team.

I often talked about that topic over the last 20+ years with my family and friends, as well as other people, and I came to the conclusion, from God's Word and those conversations, that it's not for me to fully understand why the punishment has to be so severe. My basic understanding is that Heaven cannot be occupied by those who didn't want to play on Jesus' team to begin with. So, why would they end up being in Heaven with the team they personally chose to not be a part of? If you've ever bought a home, you understand how important it is to make sure the neighborhood is safe, especially if you have young children. You don't want to be in a neighborhood where there's drive-by shootings, or drug dealings going on at the corner of your block. Unfortunately, that's the only choice many people have. That doesn't mean that everyone who lives in that neighborhood is bad, it just means that there's some evil people living there, who are making it a not so nice neighborhood to live in. You can also move into a neighborhood that starts out great, but then slowly turns into a dangerous neighborhood to live in.

> Galatians 5:9: *"A little yeast works through the whole batch of dough."*

If Heaven is going to be a great place to live, then we need to trust Jesus who knows who to let in, and who to keep out. I say this with a heavy heart, knowing that I have lost loved ones in my life, that I wasn't quite sure if they had made the decision to make Jesus Christ their personal Lord and Savior of their life. But I no longer allow myself to get bogged down in wondering who's going to make it to heaven. I just keep trying to focus in on making sure that I'm doing my best to walk as Jesus walked, and to help my family do the same by setting the example for them to follow. I try to recruit as many people to "Team Jesus" as possible, without relying on my own strength and judgement. Because the Bible says that we all fall short of the glory of God. That we have all sinned and that no one is righteous in the sight of God, except for those who have accepted the mercy and forgiveness that comes with making Jesus the Lord/Coach of their life.

The bottom-line is that you can't earn it. And if you can't earn it, then you need to accept being saved as a gift. If you've ever given a gift to someone, you can fully understand what I'm saying. You give it because you obviously wanted to give that gift. You wanted to give it because you care about the person you gave it to. But you weren't expecting anything back, except for them to love you and to be your friend. That's what Jesus wants from us. He wants to be our friend, and He wants to be our Savior. The benefits of Jesus, being your Savior, is that you're saved from eternal separation from God. When we take our last breath, the Bible says that we'll be judged. And that Jesus is going to be next to us before the judgement throne, like a lawyer defending His client.

> Revelation 20:12 *"And I saw the dead, great and small, standing before the throne, and books were opened. Another book was opened, which is the book of life. The dead were judged according to what they had done as recorded in the books."*

Are you ready for the Good News? The Good News is that, whatever is found in those books about the life you and I have lived, however bad it may be, it doesn't matter. The only thing that matters is whether you accepted Jesus Christ as your personal Lord and Savior, and did your very best to live your life for Him. Did you rely on His strength, or your own? Did you allow Him to be the Coach of your life? If you did, then you relied on His wisdom, and His Words, to show you how to live your life. Not by feelings, but by the Truth, in His playbook for your life, which puts an end to all arguments, of what is right, and what is wrong. I'm not here to judge anyone, because that's God's job. But I'm here to tell you, that if you're confused about what's right and wrong in this world, you don't need to look anywhere else other than the Bible to clear up the confusion in your mind. Once you believe that it's our creators manual for our lives, and that it is incorruptible and fully reliable, then you can stop wondering about how to live your life, and simply start living without doubt, according to what God's Word says is "THE TRUTH."

As mentioned in the beginning of this book, I told you that before I became a Christian, I wasn't sure if the Bible was 100%, without a doubt, the incorruptible Word of God. But when I believed, I started realizing things like … "If God could suspend this giant ball we call the Earth in midair with an invisible force we call gravity, then couldn't He make sure He leaves us humans whom He created with an owner's manual, that we could trust as a reliable guide, to live our lives, and explain our existence?" Here's another thought to ponder. There are some who believe in the Big Bang Theory, where nothing was created on purpose, but everything was created by accident based on a big explosion of some sort. So, based on the intricacies of all species of animals, and us humans, from the design of the eye to the nose, or even the vocal chords that allow people to sing and speak, could this be an accident? Or what about the unique design of a fish, or a bird flying in the sky with the aerodynamic wings it has?

If all of that was created by a bang, then shouldn't we be able to throw a stack of one thousand pages of paper, each containing random letters that are from the English language and in an order that spells no intelligible words, and throw it against a wall and have it form itself and the words into Webster's dictionary? We can't even picture that happening can we? How about the sun, the moon, and the seasons?

How everything is ordered just right, to make sure that us earthlings don't get burned up by the sun. If the temperature and course of the sun were off by just a few degrees, we could get burned up into stubble. So, enough said on whether the Bible is 100% reliable, and whether we can trust it to be the Book that we live our lives by. The biggest benefit to having Jesus as our life Coach and personal Savior, is that our eyes are opened to the fact that the Bible is His book we can live by, and live in victory for the rest of our lives on this earth. His book can lead us to eventually be in Heaven with Him for all eternity.

Yesterday Is History, Tomorrow Is a Mystery, And Today Is a Gift ...That's Why It's Called "The Present"

If life is referred to as, "The Game of Life," then we must learn to understand that any playing time we have been given, is a true blessing. It's like a player on a team, who is sitting on the bench wishing they could get in the game. I think of an old song by John Fogerty, from the 80's called, "Centerfield." The main line in the song is, "Put me in coach, I'm ready to play today." As a player on any team, the players are always wanting to get in the game. You and I are in the game right now. Is our head in the game? Is our heart in the game? If not, we need to understand that today is a gift, and that's why it's called the present. The best players, on a sports team, feel that they're being given a gift by the coach, when he puts them in the game, and gives them the opportunity to play. We need to look at the game of life in the same way. We need to be grateful for "The Present," known as today.

I Did the Fire Walk, But He Walked on Water

Back in 2004 I went to a 3-day success/motivational seminar. The main highlight of the seminar was that we would be taught how to walk over 12 feet of burning hot coals with our bare feet, without getting burned. I told a couple of friends of mine a few days before I went to the seminar, about the fire walk, and one of them started telling me that I wouldn't be able to do it. That it was impossible. But of course, I told him that I'd let him know if he was right after the seminar. We were supposed to get there on a Friday night at 5:00 pm to check in, and by midnight that same night, we would all be prepared to successfully walk over the burning hot coals without getting any burns or blisters.

So, it all came down to a couple of things that we needed to do in-order-to successfully do the fire walk. That seminar cost me around $1,000 dollars at the time, which was a lot more money than it is today based on today's cost of living. But fortunately for you, I'm going to tell you how I was taught to successfully do the fire walk. HUGE DISCLAIMER … I want to make it fully clear, that in no way, shape, or form, am I recommending that you or anyone you know, tries to do the fire walk on your own. It should be done in a professionally monitored setting, with an ambulance, and paramedics present. So, consider this a legal disclaimer, making it fully clear, that I'm telling you to, NOT go out and attempt this on your own, or with your friends. Now that we have that taken care of, I can tell you how I, along with hundreds of other people, successfully did, what most would say is impossible. These were the principles we were all taught in-order-to do this. We were told, that the mind can do anything, IF it believes that what it's attempting to do is possible. Remember the Scripture I mentioned to you, where Jesus said in -

> Mark 9:23: *"If you can?' said Jesus, "Everything is possible for one who believes."*

Did you hear what Jesus said? EVERYTHING IS POSSIBLE FOR ONE WHO BELIEVES. So, first, and foremost, we had to believe that we could do it. Second, we had to get ourselves into what is called a peak state. The example we were given at the seminar, was a baseball player up to bat in game 7 of the World Series … in the bottom of the 9th, with 2 outs, and bases loaded, and the batter up at the plate representing the winning run. We were asked to answer, what kind of state the batter at the plate would have to be in, to come through in the clutch. What would his physical and mental state have to be like, on a scale of 1 to 10? And, of course the answer would be for him to have a chance at getting a hit, or even a grand slam, he would have to be at a 10, to have his best chance at coming through in the clutch. So, that's the kind of state, those of us who were about to walk over the burning hot coals, had to be in, to successfully walk across the 12 feet of burning hot coals without getting burns or blisters on our feet. We would have to be in our absolute best peak state.

We were taught what was known as a power move. It was a move that instantly anchored us back into our most powerful state, by simply doing that move. The move was anchored into us during the repeated moments of feeling unstoppable at the seminar. My power move was to clench my right fist with all my strength, and to lower my arm, and clenched fist, while confidently saying "YES," with as much intensity, power, and passion as possible. And to repeat that power move, until I felt I was in my peak state. We had to get the power move conditioned into our body and mind, by listening to powerful, loud music, and by feeling the emotions of strength and power. And that allowed us to recall that feeling of power, at any given moment. The last step was to stand at the beginning of the 12 feet of burning hot coals, and to look up, instead of focusing down at the burning hot coals. The moment we started walking over the burning hot coals, we were to say to ourselves, what was described to us in our minds, as cool moss. The soft and green moss, that grows on the rocks in the ocean, or other bodies of water.

So, these were the steps. Do your power move, and get into a peak state. Second, look up, and keep repeating, "cool moss, cool moss, cool moss," until you completed walking over the entire 12 feet of burning hot coals. At the very end, there was someone with a hose to immediately hose off our feet, to make sure there weren't any burning hot coals stuck on the bottom of them. There were ambulances lined up and ready to go. There were about 20 different lines of people waiting for their turn to do the fire walk. As each line was doing the walk, there were people screaming and crying because not everyone was successful. Fortunately, I completed it, successfully, without a single burn or blister on my feet … it was truly an amazing experience. I wasn't the only one who did it successfully. There were many who succeeded. And while that's extremely impressive, Jesus coached one of His players into doing something even more impressive.

Jesus coached a guy named Peter into walking on warer. And I'm yet to meet anyone who has successfully done what Peter did. Though, I did see a tv episode of "Mind Freak" on A&E, where Criss Angel, "The Magician," fooled everyone, with his magical illusion trick, into thinking that he had successfully walked on water. And then he shows you how he did it. He basically had a path of elevated glass steps, just below the surface of the water, that he walked on. Somehow, I don't think Jesus used the same technique. So, let's get into how Jesus coached Peter, to successfully walk on water.

Matthew 14:25-28

> ²⁵Shortly before dawn Jesus went out to them, walking on the lake. ²⁶When the disciples saw him walking on the lake, they were terrified. "It's a ghost," they said, and cried out in fear.
>
> ²⁷But Jesus immediately said to them: "Take courage! It is I. Don't be afraid."
>
> ²⁸"Lord, if it's you," Peter replied, "tell me to come to you on the water."

That's a pretty cool story huh? What makes it even cooler is that it's a true story, if you believe what the Bible says. But here's the rest of the story.

Matthew 14:29-31

> ²⁹"Come," he said. Then Peter got down out of the boat, walked on the water, and came toward Jesus. ³⁰But when he saw the wind, he was afraid and, beginning to sink, cried out, "Lord, save me!"
>
> ³¹Immediately Jesus reached out his hand and caught him. "You of little faith," he said, "why did you doubt?"

This story obviously blows away the fire walk. Not to mention that in the fire walk, our teacher wasn't standing still on the burning hot coals with his bare feet, or even his shoes, while teaching us how to walk over to him with our bare feet. Think about how amazing it would be to literally walk on water. I believe that if it's in the Bible, we can count on it being true. We can see here, from what Jesus said to Peter, that he was being coached into walking on the water. He was told to have faith. He was told to have courage, and to not be afraid. And he was asked why he had doubt about being able to walk on the water. Keep in mind, that Peter had just seen Jesus walking on the water successfully, because Jesus walked out on the lake towards the boat that Peter and Jesus' other disciples were in. Jesus is the ultimate player Coach. He has never asked us to do anything that He himself wasn't already doing, or hadn't already done. This story epitomizes the saying, "Stepping Out on Faith."

My Grandmother Told Me That Jesus Physically Appeared to Her

> Luke 8:43: *⁴³And a woman was there who had been subject to bleeding for twelve years, but no one could heal her. ⁴⁴She came up behind him and touched the edge of his cloak, and immediately her bleeding stopped.*

You and I live in a time where Jesus isn't always physically seen in front of us, like Peter had seen when he walked on water. However, my grandmother on my father's side, told me that she saw Jesus appear to her at the end of her hospital bed, after the priest had come in with the doctors, to speak the last rites of passage over her while she was in a coma. She was bleeding internally, and the doctors couldn't stop the bleeding. So, they gave up on her, and called the priest in. My grandmother had over 6 kids at the time, and the youngest was still in diapers. She told me that she could hear the priest reading her last rites of passage, and immediately started praying to Jesus, that if He would heal her, and let her live to raise her children, that she would serve others, and live the rest of her life for Him.

What she told me next has helped me to have faith throughout my whole life, because of her incredibly powerful, personal testimony of seeing Jesus. She said that Jesus appeared to her at the end of her hospital bed, and had a long flowing purple robe on, like a King would be wearing, along with a gold like necklace/breast plate. How fitting, since

He is known as "The King of Kings." She said that His appearance was more glorious than she could've ever imagined. So basically, she had just finished having her last rites prayed over her. And as she heard the priest speaking words of death and defeat over her, she was praying to Jesus for victory over death. She said that immediately after the priest left, and as she lay there bleeding to death in her bed, she said that Jesus appeared to her at the foot of her hospital bed, and motioned with His arms, for her to get up out of the bed. Once she got up out of the bed and started walking towards Him, He then disappeared. She then proceeded to walk out of her hospital room, and into the hospital hallway, where the nurses saw her, and went to get the doctor. They all expected her to be dead any minute. When the doctor showed up and re-examined her, he noticed that the bleeding had stopped, and she was completely healed.

She went on to raise all her kids to adulthood, and lived over an additional 50 years, with incredibly good health, and made good on her promise to Him. She was still driving her car into her late 70's. My grandmother made good on her promise to serve others by volunteering her time at the children's hospitals in Chicago, Illinois. She also worked full time as a nurse's aide at a nursing home, where she took care of the elderly who were sick. She also helped my dad to raise my brothers and I, by driving over to our house just about every Monday thru Friday morning at about 6 am to cook, clean, and get us off to school. She even helped pay for me to go to college, and helped me to buy the sound system for me to go out and play live with my band. She was grateful to say the least, that Jesus came into her life, and showed her appreciation to Him by making good on her promise to Him, that she would serve others. Even though you and I may not have seen the physical hand of Jesus reaching out to us, we can sense his spiritual hand lifting us up, whether it's through Him strengthening us with His supernatural and unexplainable power to do something, or to help us go through dark times.

Hebrews 1:14 "Are not all angels ministering spirits sent to serve those who will inherit salvation?"

Darren Taylor

I love that Scripture because it says that the angels are sent to serve those who will inherit salvation. All of us on "Team Jesus," have our own personal guardian angel. And you thought that was just something you saw in the movies. If you believe His Word, then you now know that angels are real, and that they're part of His team. But our culture depicts them as cute little figurines that are sold at a gift shop. Sleep well my friend, because most likely, Jesus has angels camped around you, and your entire family at this very moment.

We Score Victories in Life by Getting into The Faith Zone

> Hebrews 11:1 *"Now faith is confidence in what we hope for and assurance about what we do not see."*

Everything we do, when it comes to being coached by Jesus, involves having faith. We're all very familiar with the concept of having faith in ourselves, or in other humans. But when it comes to having faith in Jesus, who most of us haven't seen, it becomes much more difficult to have that faith. But the Bible says that without faith, it's impossible to please God.

> Hebrews 11:6 *"And without faith it is impossible to please God, because anyone who comes to him must believe that he exists and the he rewards those who earnestly seek him."*

That Scripture is one of the most important verses in the entire Bible. At the end, the Scripture says that he rewards those who earnestly seek Him. There are only a few different ways to seek God. But I think the best way we can seek God, and pick His brain, is to read His Word. And if you believe the Bible is His word, then you can hang on every word you read in the Bible. But one of the many things the enemy likes to do, when it comes to God's Word, is to distort the truth, by making believers think that God's Word is corrupted by man and cannot be trusted. The enemy wants us to believe that we can't fully understand it, and that it's too complicated and too difficult for anyone other than a priest or preacher. That couldn't be farther from the truth. Let's read in this next Scripture, to see what God says about that.

2 Peter 3:16, He writes the same way in all His letters, speaking in them of these matters. His letters contain some things that are hard to understand, which ignorant and unstable people distort, as they do the other Scriptures, to their own destruction.

Peter clearly says that some of God's Word is hard to understand, but the enemy sees the opening in the defense, and takes the opportunity to run with that lie. The bottom-line is that we need to have faith, that we can even understand God's Word. Fortunately, He gives us His Holy Spirit to help us understand His Word. But it truly is all about faith, and our goal is to always have faith.

The Hall of Faith

God doesn't put His star players in the "Hall of Fame," BUT He does put them in the "Hall of Faith." And the reason He does that, is because the most important ingredient involved in pleasing Him, is Faith.

Hebrews 11:7-13

> *[7]"By faith Noah, when warned about things not yet seen, in holy fear built an ark to save his family. By his faith, he condemned the world and became heir of the righteousness that is in keeping with faith."*
>
> *[8]"By faith Abraham, when called to go to a place he would later receive as his inheritance, obeyed and went, even though he did not know where he was going. [9]By faith he made his home in the promised land like a stranger in a foreign country; he lived in tents, as did Isaac and Jacob, who were heirs with him of the same promise. [10]For he was looking forward to the city with foundations, whose architect and builder is God. [11]And by faith even Sarah, who was past childbearing age, was enabled to bear children because she considered him faithful who had made the promise. [12]And so from this one man, and he as good as dead, came descendants as numerous as the stars in the sky and as countless as the sand on the seashore. [13]All these people were still living by faith when they died. They did*

> *not receive the things promised; they only saw them and welcomed them from a distance, admitting that they were foreigners and strangers on earth."*

Though that's a long Scripture, I wanted to include it, so you can see how there is indeed, a "Hall of Faith" in the Bible. We can look at the people God has put in "The Hall of Faith" to understand how important God says that faith is, with regards to the players, He considers worth mentioning. So, where would you say that your faith is right now, regarding Jesus Christ being real, and His word being the playbook you can fully trust, and live your life by? On a scale of 1 to 10, where would you rank it? If you're currently feeling like you're at the level of an atheist, that's ok. Just keep reading this book, and I'll help you to have more faith in "The Greatest Coach of All Time."

I know what it's like to go through the darkest of dark times in my own personal life. And I know what it's like to go through that dark tunnel, and to reach the light at the end of the tunnel. Have you ever seen the movie, "The Shawshank Redemption?" If not, I highly recommend you go and see it. One of the cousins of the word "Faith," is "Hope." The ending scene in "The Shawshank Redemption" is incredible! It involves a Scripture from God's Word. I won't say any more about it, but if you get nothing out of this book, other than a recommendation to see one of the greatest hope inspiring movies of all time, then I can feel good about that. After watching the movie, you will be overflowing with hope. My hope is to really help you to understand, that you already have access to "The Greatest Coach of All Time." He's waiting for you to trust Him to be your Coach. The opposing team doesn't want you to have Him as your Head Coach, because they know that once you have Jesus as your Head Coach, it's game over for them. They know that you'll be on the team that has already won. But the question is, which team will you choose to play on? "Team Jesus" or "Team Satan"? It's going to take a lot of faith on your part to choose to play on "Team Jesus," but your faith will be richly rewarded.

He Blesses and Disciplines Those He Loves and Those Who Love Him

> 1 Corinthians 2:9 *"However, as it is written: 'What no eye has seen, what no ear has heard, and what no human mind has conceived,' are the things God has prepared for those who love Him."*

Isn't that an awesome Scripture? All we need to do is love Him to partake in what He's prepared for us. Because He loves us, He also disciplines us. Just like our earthly parents are supposed to. You heard it said that some coaches treat their players like their own son or daughter, right?

> Hebrews 12:8 *"If you are not disciplined. and everyone undergoes discipline, then you are not legitimate, not true sons and daughters at all."*

Were you disciplined by your parents or whoever raised you? I was raised from the age of 7, by my dad and my grandma. My parents divorced when I was 7, and two of my brothers who were 3 and 8 moved with me from living with my mom in Arizona, to moving to Illinois, to live with my dad. My mom gave my brothers and I a choice as to who we wanted to live with after moving to Arizona, and we chose to move back with our dad in Illinois to be back where most of our friends and family lived. Fortunately, my mom would fly out to see us as much as she could. Whenever she came to visit, it was like a week long celebration where she would make us our favorite foods and take us out to do lots of fun things. She's a great mom, and I'm grateful to have her in my life to this day. The divorce was very difficult for her, and so was her sacrifice to let us live with our dad.

As mentioned earlier, my grandma who saw, and was miraculously healed by Jesus, used to come over just about every morning at about 6 am to clean up, cook for us, and do laundry, along with getting us ready for school. I would be laying in bed trying to milk every minute of sleep, before having to get up and go to school. My grandma would have her carpet sweeper, that she would use throughout the whole house, and it would always wake me up when she would carpet sweep past my room. My dad wasn't into spanking us, and didn't really like to discipline us, the way the Bible says we should be disciplined. So, we pretty much worked everything out by talking about it. But the only problem was that my dad didn't read the Bible, and didn't know exactly what it said about raising kids. I joined "Team Jesus," when I was 25 years old, and found out when I started reading God's Word, that my dad was going off what he thought was best for us according to pop culture.

The Party's Over

My brothers and I were raised on watching Cheech And Chong movies, where they would smoke marijuana all day and night, and seem to be having the best time anyone could possibly have. Once I became a teenager, my dad let me have huge parties at our house, starting when I was 16. He would buy the kegs of beer and the plastic solo cups, and I would charge $3 dollars per person to be at my party. Once they gave me the 3 bucks, I gave them the cup, and it was party time. It was like owning a bar at the age of 16. Obviously, it wasn't something that any parent should have supported their kid in doing. I mentioned earlier that my dad was a great man, who happened to have an addiction to alcohol, and prescription pills. Unfortunately, he never completely overcame his addictions. I learned a lot about addictions by watching him struggle his whole life with two of the most destructive addictions anyone could have.

My dad had an incredibly great sense of humor, and a lot of people called him "Mr. Brady," because he looked a lot like the "Mr. Brady" on "The Brady Bunch" tv show. He used to have straight hair when he was younger, but when the disco craze hit in the seventies, so did the "get a perm" craze. Getting back to the parties I would have in high school, I was known as the kid who had the biggest and best parties. I share this story with you, because I think it's important to understand where someone has been, to understand where they are in the present, with their life and beliefs. So, the bottom-line is that I was on the road of partying at an early age, and ended up taking what I saw, from the

Cheech and Chong movies, along with my experience as a teenager who had great parties, and became a guy who was into sex, drugs and rock and roll.

When I got out of high school, I started singing with different bands, and started my own Karaoke company. I would go to different bars, and be the host of Karaoke night. I would also DJ weddings. Life was one big party for me, from the age of 16 to 25. At the age of 25, I ended up impregnating my girlfriend at the time who was also the drummer in my band. A year later, she would become my wife of 13 years. After having 3 wonderful sons, we would divorce after 13 years of marriage. Unfortunately, during the course, of our marriage, she ended up going back to the drug addictions and depression that she had, before I met her. I ended up being a single father of our 3 boys. About a year after our divorce, she unfortunately overdosed. I could write an entire book, on drug and alcohol addictions, and how it ruins your life, and God's plans for your life. Perhaps I'll save that for another book.

I want to get back to how Jesus holds us accountable to following, "His Game Changing Playbook." It's impossible to follow the Bible, or a playbook, if you don't know what it says. I didn't start getting into what the Bible said, until I was 25. So, everything I thought I knew about life, and the truth, was all about what I thought was right and wrong. But the truth is, I was very wrong, about what I thought the Bible said. The good news is that once you know what the Bible says, Jesus helps you to be able to do what it says. He gives you His Holy Spirit to guide you, and to help you do what His Word says. He's a Coach that doesn't just tell you what to do, He helps you every step of the way. The following Scripture is a promise you can count on.

> John 14:26 *"But the Advocate, the Holy Spirit, whom the Father will send in my name, will teach you all things and will remind you of everything I have said to you."*

I don't know about you, but I think that's an amazing gift, that Jesus says we're going to receive when we make Him our Coach. He says that The Holy Spirit will teach us all things, and remind us of everything that Jesus has said to us. It's kind of like the quarterback who has the speaker and microphone built into his helmet. He can hear what plays the offensive coach is telling him to run. He can also communicate directly with the coach. When I think of Jesus being our Coach, that's exactly the way I look at being able to communicate with Him. We are able, to communicate with Him through prayer. And He answers us with His "Holy Spirit," by guiding us, and speaking to us in a way, that we can feel in our souls. You may have heard different Christians say, that God spoke to them. Not in audible words, but in a way that they could just hear and feel in their soul. This is what "The Holy Spirit" does. And that's how Jesus holds us accountable to following His Word. He guides us to get back on track when we need it. He guides our feelings and emotions which can be compared to having a gut feeling, about what you should do, regarding decisions in your life.

From Bitter to Better. Jesus Turned Water into Wine and He Can Turn Your Lemons into Lemonade

Have you ever made lemonade growing up as a kid? The kind where you had to add sugar to it? I remember those times as a kid very well. I was a lemonade and Kool Aid making fool. We didn't have much soda around the house but we always had Kool Aid, or some form of lemonade. There were the little packets where you had to add sugar, and there were also the containers that already had the sugar mixed in. When I would make lemonade where I had to add the sugar, I would put some sugar in, and then taste it, to make sure it was sweet enough. I would keep adding in the sugar until it tasted just right. Sometimes I would put way too much sugar and I wouldn't want to drink it.

I'm sure you've heard before, that Jesus turned water into wine. But just in case you haven't, you can read all about His wine making skills in:

> John 2:9-10 *"And the master of the banquet tasted the water that had been turned into wine. He did not realize where it had come from, though the servants who had drawn the water knew. Then he called the bridegroom aside and said, "Everyone brings out the choice wine first and then the cheaper wine after the guests have had too much to drink, but you have saved the best till now."*

Notice how it says that the best wine has been saved for the last. That's what Jesus does for us. He'll let us have our life that we have created by our own best choices. Then, He'll let us get bitter about our lives that we have created with our own free will. But when Jesus comes along, He'll take the lemons in our lives, and turn them into lemonade. He'll add the sugar and sweetness that's been missing. It doesn't matter how far along we are in our lives. Jesus will still take our bitter life and make it better. Some of the lemons that can come at us in life, would be divorce, death of a loved one, being broke, getting news of a terminal illness, and too many other lemons to name. Jesus wants us to convert the bitter lemons that come into our lives, into sweet lemonade, by being grateful. He wants us to know that no matter how bad our situation is, someone has always got it much worse. I know from personal experience that being grateful isn't always easy. One of my favorite preachers says that when we complain, we will remain, but when we praise, we will be raised. So, the fact is, complaining is the ingredient to life's lemonade that adds more bitterness to your life. And praise is the equivalent of adding sugar to your lemonade that makes life sweet.

Have you ever known someone who complains all the time? To the point where when you're around them, you get discouraged and depressed, just from talking to them on the phone for a few minutes? I want you to think about who that special someone is, that your friends with, or a family member of. Analyze the last few conversations you've had with them, and see if you can find anything positive or encouraging that they shared with you, the last few times you spoke with them. Now think about their life. Would you say they have a bitter life, or a sweet life? I think you know the answer to that question. And by the way, I don't think anyone would say that bitter sweet lemonade tastes good. We need to guard our own lemonade. Because when we let people complain to us constantly, what we're really doing is, we're letting them add their bitterness to our lemonade.

Do you remember the movie "Forrest Gump?" If so, then perhaps you also remember the scene where he's shoving pieces of assorted chocolates into his mouth. While he's chewing it, he says, "My mama always said that life is like a box of chocolates, you never know what you're gonna get." I have to disagree with that. Nowadays you can look underneath the box top, and you can see the chart that tells you what chocolates are in the box. You need to get good at identifying which people in your life, are the kinds of chocolates you like. And you need to guard your lemonade of life, because letting the wrong people around you will turn it bitter. Fortunately, Jesus has a "Game Changing Playbook for Your Comeback."

Jesus' Favorite Play Call, is to Go Deep

> Proverbs 20:5 *"The purposes of a person's heart are deep waters, but one who has insight draws them out."*

Every football coach has their favorite plays that they like to call. I believe that Jesus' favorite play call is to go deep. He wants us to look deep into our own hearts, and truly do some soul searching. He wants us to analyze our intentions about every situation. He wants us to make sure we are following "His Playbook" for our lives, and not our own. Most importantly, the above Scripture says that the purposes of a person's heart are deep waters. So, we can't be shallow people if we're going to have success. We can't wear a mask and play church. We need to be real with ourselves, and real with other people. Reading the defense, is similar to knowing how to read people. We need to become good at knowing if someone's being fake or authentic. The quality of your life depends on it. I always compare fakeness to the movie, "The Stepford Wives." That's the movie where the wives all act like robots … fake as can be. I think we're supposed to be honest with ourselves about what our purpose is in life, along with what our intentions are.

Do you remember earlier on, when I mentioned to you, that Jesus wants us to be a fisher of people? If so, then as a fisherman, or a fisherwoman, we must use the right bait. You'll either use live bait, or a lure, that looks like live bait. Either way, your bait must look attractive to the fish if you're going to catch it. From my personal experience, I know that either bait works, but I think that live bait works the best. And that's because it's real. Now if a fish can spot something that's fake, do you think that maybe another human can detect if a person is being fake? I've been accused throughout my life of saying things that most people wouldn't say. And some people, who have been around me throughout the years, have felt a bit uncomfortable at times, and even turned red in the face, as their reaction to what I said to someone in their presence. I have toned it down throughout the last twenty years or so, due to wanting to be sure I don't turn someone away from wanting to be on "Team Jesus," because they may be offended by what I might say.

I learned that people relate much better to someone who they believe is being completely real. If you were to be more vulnerable, and let people know the struggles you've had throughout your life, along with the sin that you used to struggle with, but have overcome, they might share with you that they're currently struggling with the same sin that you shared with them. Your personal testimony will give them hope that if you were able to overcome that struggle, they can do the same.

I opened-up a little bit with you about my marriage to my first wife. And I'm going to open-up a bit more with you right now, because I'm hoping it might encourage you to keep the faith in your marriage, or whatever circumstance you find yourself in right now. I mentioned to you how my life had become sex, drugs and rock and roll at about the age of 16. My lifestyle had finally caught up with me at the age of 25. I had met a great guitarist who had come out to one of my Karaoke shows that I ran on a weekly basis. He and I had talked about forming a band. We would need a drummer for the band, and he had mentioned to me that his sister was a great drummer, and that she was moving to Illinois from New Jersey in about a week. He also mentioned that she was coming straight from rehab to move here. I asked my friend if she was pretty, and he said that she was beautiful. He said that her 21st birthday was in about a week, so I told him to bring her out to my show to celebrate her birthday. So, he brought her out, and after meeting her, we hit it off. Six months later, I got her pregnant. We decided to keep the baby, even though neither of us were Christians at the time. I just simply didn't believe in abortion, and decided to man up and have our kid. So, I proposed to her and told her we should get married, and take care of our unborn child that was on the way. Long story short, we moved in together, and after our son was 1, we ended up getting married.

Shortly after getting married, the anxiety, depression and drug addictions resurfaced for my wife. I was still into smoking pot at the time, and my musical dreams went up in smoke. We started having some very serious marriage problems, and both of us ended up reaching out to Jesus and finding Him through the major problems we were having. Fast forward to us having a total of 3 awesome sons. I gave my life to Jesus and gave up the weed. Though my wife and I were heavily involved in a church, and even became Bible study leaders and zone leaders in that church. We ended up leaving that church after 7 years of ups-and-downs, only to realize that the church we were a part of, was more like a cult, filled with legalism, that could only be compared to the Pharisees and Sadducees of Jesus' time. With that said, I believe many of the members of that church were good people who wanted to know Jesus. But like myself, they were deceived by the opposing team into thinking that their righteousness could be achieved by their human effort, rather than by the sacrifice and price that was paid by Jesus, when he willingly gave His life on the cross for us, so that we could be made righteous before God.

I don't judge the people I went to church with, but I do want to mention my personal experience, in case you or someone you might know, is in the same bad situation that I brought my family into. So, when I talk to you about legalism in the next chapter, you'll know exactly where I'm coming from. Early on in my walk with Jesus, I wouldn't have wanted to share my personal life with anyone. But I now realize, that it's those very same types of true stories and testimonies that I had heard, that made me believe, that whatever I was struggling with, could be overcome by having faith in Jesus. As I mentioned earlier, unfortunately, the story of my first marriage, ended with my wife being overtaken by her addictions and depression, and she ended up losing her battle to addiction and depression about a year after our divorce. Our marriage had lasted about 13 years, and our 3 amazing boys came as a result from our marriage. If you're like I used to be, you might not want to hear anything more about what I need to say about being a Christian, or about Jesus, because you might be judging me as a failure in marriage, or a bad Christian. Fortunately, I took to heart what Jesus said in Matthew 7:1-5, and realized that I was wrong to judge other Christians, with the legalistic arrogance, that I was struggling with.

Judging Others

Matthew 7:1-5 ¹"Do not judge, or you too will be judged. ²For in the same way you judge others, you will be judged, and with the measure you use, it will be measured to you."

³"Why do you look at the speck of sawdust in your brother's eye and pay no attention to the plank in your own eye? ⁴How can you say to your brother, 'Let me take the speck out of your eye,' when all the time there is a plank in your own eye? ⁵You hypocrite, first take the plank out of your own eye, and then you will see clearly to remove the speck from your brother's eye."

As I mentioned earlier, after my first marriage, I ended up being a single father of our 3 boys. My youngest was only 3 years old at the time. Not long after my first marriage, I ended up remarrying an amazing woman of God, who happened to have 3 kids of her own, and we ended up becoming, "The Real-life Brady Bunch Meets the Partridge Family Gone Country." Throughout the entire struggle of my first marriage, I know that Jesus was there, through His Holy Spirit, to coach me through the pain and struggles my wife, my children, and myself, ended up going through. Even as I write this personal information about my own life, I have thoughts of not sharing this with you. The old me always wanted to pretend that I had the perfect life, and the perfect family. The opposing team wants us to believe that it's better to be fake, and act like you're the perfect family, just like the "Brady Bunch" tv show. But if you're reading

Darren Taylor

this, then you obviously know, that I decided to pull the skeletons out of my closet for the whole world to see, so I might be able to encourage you to keep going, no matter how bad your situation might be. If you keep believing, and never give up, Jesus will turn your bitter into better.

What's the Goal?

Philippians 3:12-14

> *[12]"Not that I have already obtained all this, or have already arrived at my goal, but I press on to take hold of that for which Christ Jesus took hold of me. [13]Brothers and sisters, I do not consider myself yet to have taken hold of it. But one thing I do: Forgetting what is behind and straining toward what is ahead, [14] I press on toward the goal to win the prize for which God has called me heavenward in Christ Jesus."*

I believe the goal is to forget your past, and to move forward towards the goal. Jesus wants us to take off the grave clothes, and to put on the great clothes! In the past, I used to complicate things. I would beat myself up over my past mistakes, and I would convince myself, that I needed to continue to punish myself, and deprive myself, of any new successes, due to my past failures. I had people in my life who weren't willing to forgive me for my mistakes, so I thought I couldn't forgive myself either. I thought I had to carry out their punishment for me on behalf of those who wanted to punish me. Fortunately, I was able to forgive myself, when I realized that Jesus had forgiven me, even if others were unwilling to do so.

Satan and all his players don't want you or me to ever be forgiven. They want us to go to hell with them. They love it when you or I feel unforgiven and defeated. And they hate the fact that Jesus has forgiven us and has taken the punishment in our place so that we could be fully forgiven. Isn't that awesome? I don't know about you, but I had a hard time being happy when I was beating myself up, on a daily basis, over my past sins and mistakes. One of my favorite preachers said to his congregation, "Do you know why they make the rearview mirror so small and the windshield so big?" It's because you're not supposed to focus in on what's behind, you're supposed to look ahead and see the big picture of your future. That's why the windshield is so big, and the rearview mirror is so small." I think we should take his advice and focus in on what's ahead rather than staring in the rearview mirror so much. We should look at the past, but not live in the past. Your goal is in front of you. In soccer, there are two goals. One in front of you, and one behind you. Which goal are you focusing in on? Forgiveness is the main theme or message that Jesus wants us to understand and put into practice. In a song, you are supposed to have a catchy chorus, or a hook. I believe that "Forgiveness" is the hook, and that Jesus wants us to catch on to that hook. Is there someone you need to forgive from the heart? Maybe even yourself? If so, don't put it off any longer.

You Have Been Pardoned. Now Leave Your Self-Imposed Prison

This next true story is about a woman caught in adultery. Reading this helped me greatly in understanding that Jesus set me free from holding myself prisoner of my past mistakes. It's a bit long. BUT this book isn't about my own personal opinion about what you should do with your past mistakes or sin. It's about Jesus being, "The Greatest Coach of All Time." This next story is the perfect example of Jesus coaching or teaching a woman caught in the sin of adultery. Keep in mind, that this happened in front of a big crowd of people, who wanted to kill her.

John 8:2-11

> *²"At dawn He appeared again in the temple courts, where all the people gathered around Him, and He sat down to teach them. ³The teachers of the law and the Pharisees brought in a woman caught in adultery. They made her stand before the group ⁴and said to Jesus, "Teacher, this woman was caught in the act of adultery. ⁵In the Law Moses commanded us to stone such women. Now what do you say?" ⁶They were using this question as a trap, in-order to have a basis for accusing Him.*
>
> *But Jesus bent down and started to write on the ground with His finger. ⁷When they kept on questioning Him, He straightened up and said to them, "Let any one of you who*

> *is without sin be the first to throw a stone at her." ⁸Again He stooped down and wrote on the ground.*
>
> *⁹At this, those who heard began to go away one at a time, the older ones first, until only Jesus was left, with the woman still standing there. ¹⁰Jesus straightened up and asked her, "Woman, where are they? Has no one condemned you?"*
>
> *¹¹"No one, sir," she said.*
>
> *"Then neither do I condemn you,' Jesus declared." "Go now and leave your life of sin."*

This is truly an amazing, teachable moment. I've heard this story discussed in many different sermons. But I think this story gives us the formula to forgive ourselves, and to move forward in our lives, without guilt. Once we know that we have been forgiven, by Jesus, we must forgive ourselves. Jesus gives us His forgiveness as a gift. We give ourselves a gift by forgiving ourselves. Once you're right with Him, it all comes down to how you feel about yourself. The woman caught in adultery had been forgiven, but did she forgive herself? You'll notice that all the teachers of the law, and the Pharisees, wouldn't cast the first stone because they knew that they were all sinners as well. I can just hear the rocks dropping to the ground one by one, as they realized they couldn't outsmart Jesus. But what's most important here, is that Jesus tells her that He does not condemn her for her sin of adultery. But He does tell her, to go now, and leave your life of sin. So, when we ask the question of, "What is the goal?" I think it's made clear, when Jesus says to the woman, "Go now and leave your life of sin." It's important to understand, that neither you or I, are perfect, and we're sinning every day.

We are commanded to leave our life of sin. Every day is a new day, and every moment is a new chance for you and I to continue to leave our lives of sin. We are told to run away from each sin, that we're aware of.

Obviously, if we don't detect our own sin, we can't run away from it. So, the goal is to consistently be aware of our sin, and to leave it. With my experience, and background of legalism, I can tell you first hand, that the opposing team wants you to believe, that you should just quit, because your sin disqualifies you from being forgiven. Every time you sin, the enemy/accuser wants you to think that you're not forgiven. Satan wants you to think that you're an unredeemable deplorable. He's wrong!

Jesus didn't say that you won't ever sin again. He said to leave your life of sin. The problem is, when you leave your life of sin, Satan and all his demons continue to follow you, and try to tempt you to go back to playing on their team. But our Coach wants us to remember that victory is assured if we stay focused on Him, and His game plan for our lives. As-long-as we do that, we can successfully resist the temptation to go play for "The Hell City Demons" again. Jesus wants us to do our very best, by making sure that we're doing everything that we can, to rely on Him. He wants us to go out on the playing field of life, and to lay it all on the line. And during the entire game of life, He knows that the opposing team is going to play a mental, physical, spiritual, and emotional game with us. Don't fall for it.

It's A Mental Game

> Romans 12:2 *"Do not conform to the pattern of this world, but be transformed by the renewing of your mind. Then you will be able to test and approve what God's will is--his good, pleasing and perfect will."*

Every day, and every moment, we are to be transformed by the renewing of our mind. The Scripture says for us to not conform to the pattern of this world. When I think of a pattern, I think of a record, that has its pattern of grooves. It plays the same way every time. Our goal is to scratch the record pattern of this world. It's to have a different pattern than what the world teaches us. As Christians, we are called to be different. We are called to do things the way Jesus wants us to do them. His promise to us, is that if we'll do things His way, then we will win. It's His personal guarantee to us. But Satan and all his demons, want to recruit as many of Jesus' players to their losing team as possible. You've most likely heard the saying, "misery loves company." That's exactly what the opposing team wants to see happen. Since they know they're not going to win, they want as many people to be in the losers' circle with them as possible. Once again, if you're on "Team Jesus," victory is guaranteed. But there's one condition, you must never quit His team.

Get into His Groove

There's a certain groove to Jesus' game plan. He simply wants you to get into His groove. Not your own, or the opposing teams groove. If you will follow His pattern for success, it will be like being guided by your GPS navigation. Once you're in His navigation system, and are willing to be guided by Him, you'll make it to the destination He wants to lead you to. If you get off route, He'll always guide you with an alternate route to get you back on track.

> Psalm 46:10 *"Be still, and know that I am God; I will be exalted among the nations, I will be exalted in the earth."*

If you think about that Scripture, it's really, not a whole lot different than the New England Patriots winning the Super Bowl recently, with their amazing comeback. Coach Bill Belichick was exalted around the world by many, as the greatest coach ever. He was exalted, because he's the guy responsible for coaching the Patriots to victory. His team is simply following his game plan. Though it's filled with quite a few audibles, the team practices what to do, and what play to call, in every possible scenario. They're reading the defense, and they're receiving the plays that are called from different coaches, but there's only one head coach, and he gets most of the credit and most of the blame if the team loses. Jesus says that His plan for victory is guaranteed. All you need to do is to get into His groove, believe what He said, and get to know His playbook.

Jesus Likes to Call Audibles

Jesus changes up the play calling last minute on a regular basis, because His players are given free will to go with one of His plays, or to call their own. Sometimes we can get away from His playbook, and go completely against what Jesus would have wanted us to do. So, we end up messing things up. Sometimes we'll be running down the field towards the end zone, with a play that we called all on our own. It looks like that play was the right call, but then we end up fumbling the ball at the 1 yard line. Or maybe we call a pass play, and go for the Hail Mary, when we should've run the ball. It's not how it looks like the play is going, it's how the play ends up going. The enemy is trying to sack, or intercept our dreams. We end up suffering the consequences for our bad play call. It's just like having a penalty called in football. But in life, we sometimes lose more than yardage.

Sometimes our mistakes can cost us a marriage, or the relationship with one of our kids. It's like losing yardage, and continuously being penalized for 10 or 20 yards, until our back is inches away from the end zone, and a sack in the end zone is inevitable. If you have a family, it could mean that your family ends up suffering because of a foolish mistake. Such as being a fool with your finances, which could ultimately end up putting you in foreclosure, or simply causing a lot of stress and fights in your marriage. You may have had a great career and things could have kept going great, but you might have taken yourself out of the game, because your personal finances made your bills too much to stay in that career. You might end up going into a higher paying career, but it's not the type of career that you really wanted to be in. Maybe you had to switch careers, because you simply needed more money to pay all your overwhelming credit card debt, or a huge car payment, that you didn't need. Jesus is watching from the sidelines noticing how you're out of breath, and about to have a nervous breakdown, because of the play that you called for yourself. And then Jesus steps in, and calls His own play, that you didn't think was the right play, BUT it was the play that got you out of that situation and headed towards the end zone again.

His Players Are Rich, But They Pretend to Be Poor

> Proverbs 13:7 *"One person pretends to be rich, yet has nothing; another pretends to be poor, yet has great wealth."*

I personally know what it's like to be on top financially, and what it's like to be so broke that I had to scrape up change to put in the gas tank. I had to learn the hard way. I chose to be in different businesses or careers throughout my life that were cyclical. My dad would point this out to me when I would be spending money like a fool, and not saving nearly as much as I should have been, or saving any money at all. My dad would tell me to live below my means because when the cycle ends, you'll wish you had money saved. But fortunately, during those several times of getting rich, and then going broke, I finally learned my lesson, and started paying cash for everything, instead of racking up my credit card debt. If I needed to pay for a bill online, I used my debit card. I also decided to only buy things I needed so I could start saving money instead of always blowing my money.

> Proverbs 21:20 *"The wise store up choice food and olive oil, but fools gulp theirs down."*

Jesus wants us to save money instead of spending it like a fool. He wants us to operate out of plenty, instead of scarcity. The above Scripture talks about gulping down your food as opposed to making it last. That's the same way we need to look at our finances. We need to make it last.

Who Are You Playing the Game For?

Have you ever watched a major sporting event, and during the pre-game show, they are running a story about one of the players who just lost a loved one a day or so ago? And the player decided to still play in the game, even though they were recently devastated by their loss. They say, during their interviews with the press, that they have decided to still play in the game because their parent or family member would have wanted them to still play, and to move on with their life in victory, instead of sitting at home discouraged and defeated. I've seen many games with that situation. Every single game that I watched, I would focus solely on how that player performed in the game. Every single time, the player dedicated the game to the loved one they lost, the player absolutely crushed it. They had the game of their life. It was always extremely exciting and inspiring to watch. They had someone they were playing the game for, and they knew why they were playing to win, rather than just for how enjoyable winning was to them. What if we played the game like that all the time? What if we were able to keep up that kind of intensity and focus on winning for someone else in our life that we love? And what if that person wasn't dead, but they were at home waiting for you at the end of a long day of work? I think you know where I'm going with this.

We don't need to wait until someone dies to dedicate our lives to them. So right now, I would like you to think of anyone in your life who is still living, that you could dedicate your life and success to. In many people's lives, they can't think of anyone. But that's ok, because Jesus died for us on the cross, to pay the price for our sins, so that we wouldn't have to be punished for the sins in our own lives. And not only did Jesus die for us, but He was also raised from the dead on the third day. We have a Coach and a Savior who died for us, and came back to life, so that we could live with Him for all eternity. I believe that He is worthy of dedicating the game to. But we should also dedicate winning the game to our wife, children or our mother and father; or even a friend who has always been there for you. We will always put in our best effort if we're doing something for someone else. But if you're only playing for yourself, there's a good chance you're only putting in half the effort that you could if you made it about someone else. It just feels good to do something for someone else. This also relates to having a great boss at work, who really appreciates you and your efforts. You want to do your best for them every day you show up to work. Jesus is not only "The Greatest Coach of All Time," He's also the greatest team-mate of all time. He's a player Coach, who never asks you to do anything He hasn't already done, or isn't willing to do. I don't know of anyone who was willingly beaten, humiliated, and crucified on a cross for me, other than Jesus. Do you?

You Can't Earn a Spot on His Team

Ephesians 2:8-9 ⁸"For it is by grace you have been saved, through faith—and this is not from yourselves, it is the gift of God—⁹not by works, so that no one can boast."

Do you remember when you were in grade school or high school, and in gym class you would choose teams for kickball, softball, dodgeball or any other sport the gym teacher had you playing? I remember it like it was yesterday. I remember a few times when I ended up being chosen almost last. I never quite made it to the last one picked, but it certainly felt horrible. I always felt really, bad for the kid who was picked last. As each person was picked before me, I felt my self-esteem getting lower and lower. It was one of the worst experiences in school. We were picked based on the captain of the team seeing us play, and whether, or not he or she thought we were good. It was based on our size, and our physical abilities. We were chosen based on how high we could jump, or how fast we could run. We were also chosen on how far we could hit or throw the ball. How popular you were also played a factor.

Fortunately, those days are long gone, and my self-esteem is pretty, healthy these days, because it's no longer based on physical ability. Being on Jesus' team is a gift from Him, based on our willingness to love other people, and to make ourselves available to do, what He wants us to do. Jesus gives the invitation for everyone to be on His team, and doesn't care about anything other than their willingness to learn how to love "Him" and others. The truth is, many people say they want to be on His team, but they claim to be too busy to attend the practices and team gatherings.

THE PARABLE OF THE GREAT BANQUET

Luke 14:15-24 [15]*"When one of those at the table with Him heard this, he said to Jesus, "Blessed is the one who will eat at the feast in the kingdom of God."*

[16]*Jesus replied: "A certain man was preparing a great banquet and invited many guests. [17]At the time of the banquet he sent his servant to tell those who had been invited, 'Come, for everything is now ready.'*

[18]*"But they all alike, began to make excuses. The first said, 'I have just bought a field, and I must go and see it. Please excuse me.'*

[19]*"Another said, 'I have just bought five yoke of oxen, and I'm on my way to try them out. Please excuse me.'*

[20]*"Still another said, 'I just got married, so I can't come.'*

[21]*"The servant came back and reported this to his master. Then the owner of the house became angry and ordered his servant, 'Go out quickly into the streets and alleys of the town and bring in the poor, the crippled, the blind and the lame.'*

²² " 'Sir,' the servant said, 'what you ordered has been done, but there is still room.'

²³ "Then the master told his servant, 'Go out to the roads and country lanes and compel them to come in, so that My house will be full. ²⁴ I tell you, not one of those who were invited will get a taste of my banquet."

That's a powerful story, huh? It's so easy to think we're too busy to hang out with Jesus. I not only thought I was too busy up until the age of 25, but I thought that I had an indefinite time to accept the invitation and show up. My philosophy at the time, was to get as much sinning in before accepting the invitation from Jesus. Kind of like eating as much junk food or buffets the day before you begin your diet. I knew that once I accepted His invitation, it would be time to stop willingly sinning. But I didn't want to stop sinning, because I knew that sin was a lot of fun at the time. I didn't think about the fact that I would suffer the consequences for my actions. This is true for all of us. For example. A high school student gets into doing drugs, and it's a lot of fun. He or she gets into having sex outside of marriage. Unfortunately, once the fun and excitement of either of those sins wears off, the consequences become having a child outside of marriage, or a possible overdose and early death. Not to sound like a buzz kill for sin, but as I mentioned earlier, I ended up getting my girlfriend pregnant at the same time my music career was taking off, and my songs were being played on the radio. God turned that situation in my life from lemons into sweet lemonade. Because I wouldn't trade having my son being born for anything in the world. But dying from an overdose can't be turned into lemonade. The loved ones left behind, will always have a bitter sadness in their soul, over losing their child or family member. Fortunately, Jesus says that we can overcome temptation, and teach our kids to do the same.

James 1:13-15

> [13] "When tempted, no one should say, "God is tempting me." For God cannot be tempted by evil, nor does he tempt anyone; [14] but each person is tempted when they are dragged away by their own evil desire and enticed. [15] Then, after desire has conceived, it gives birth to sin; and sin, when it is full-grown, gives birth to death."

The reason that Scripture changed my life, is because I never realized that sin grew into death. But that's exactly what happens when you decide to continue in any sin. Sin is like a tumor to your life. As I mentioned to you before, I used to be very legalistic, and used to judge other Christians as non- Christians, if I noticed any sin in their lives. But I thank Jesus for the following Scripture, because this Scripture finally made me understand how Jesus viewed my judging of others. It changed everything for me.

Two Fingers Pointing Back at Me

Matthew 7:1-5

> *[1] "Do not judge, or you too will be judged. [2] For in the same way you judge others, you will be judged, and with the measure you use, it will be measured to you."*
>
> *[3] "Why do you look at the speck of sawdust in your brother's eye and pay no attention to the plank in your own eye? [4] How can you say to your brother, 'Let me take the speck out of your eye,' when all the time there is a plank in your own eye? [5] You hypocrite, first take the plank out of your own eye, and then you will see clearly to remove the speck from your brother's eye."*

Jesus showed me that the person I need to look at, is the guy I see in the mirror. He made me realize that when I point the finger at someone else, there's 2 of my own fingers pointing right back at me. Or 3, if you consider a pinky to be a finger. LOL. Each day, I try to focus on being grateful for the gift that I've been given, by being forgiven, and being allowed to be on His team. A team where everyone is invited to join, and a team where everyone is taught to focus in on themselves, and to stop judging their team-mates. That job is left up to God. Last time I checked, neither you or I am Him.

Everyone on His Team Is in The Starting Line Up

Unity and Diversity on His Team

1 Corinthians 12:12-20

> *[12] "Just as a body, though one, has many parts, but all its many parts form one body, so it is with Christ. [13] For we were all baptized by one Spirit so as to form one body—whether Jews or Gentiles, slave or free—and we were all given the one Spirit to drink. [14] Even so the body is not made up of one part but of many."*
>
> *[15] "Now if the foot should say, 'Because I am not a hand, I do not belong to the body,' it would not for that reason stop being part of the body. [16] And if the ear should say, 'Because I am not an eye, I do not belong to the body,' it would not for that reason stop being part of the body. [17] If the whole body were an eye, where would the sense of hearing be? If the whole body were an ear, where would the sense of smell be? [18] But in fact God has placed the parts in the body, every one of them, just as He wanted them to be. [19] If they were all one part, where would the body be? [20] As it is, there are many parts, but one body."*

I remember when my kids were all on the little league baseball team, and sometimes they would be on the bench instead of being a starting player in the game. As a parent, I always felt bad for my kids because I would look at them on the bench, and they would really look sad. But I knew that the team always had to let every kid play, and not everyone could start all the time. At that age, it wasn't always about who was the best. It was about making sure everyone got to play. After all, most everyone made it to practice, and most everyone was trying their best. I've noticed that all kids seem to always try their best. I think that's because they still believe in winning. They haven't experienced much losing in their lives at that young age, and when you haven't lost much, you have great confidence, and believe you can win just about every time.

When you're on Jesus' team, you are always in the starting lineup, and you can win every time. Even when it looks like you're losing, and even when you have experienced a setback, your setback is really a set up for your win. In the Scripture above, Jesus' team is described as a body with many parts. And all parts are as equally important. No matter what role you play, it's always a team victory. But if you're in His starting lineup, you don't have to worry about your stats, like you do in a sporting event. It's all about your efforts, and your heart, according to your own abilities combined with His. As long as you know you gave your best, and Jesus knows you gave your best, you're an All Star!!

Jesus Withdrew the Payment for Your Entry into the Race from the Blood Bank

Isaiah 53:1-12

¹ "Who has believed our message and to whom has the arm of the Lord been revealed? ²He grew up before Him like a tender shoot, and like a root out of dry ground. He had no beauty or majesty to attract us to Him, nothing in His appearance that we should desire Him. ³He was despised and rejected by mankind, a man of suffering, and familiar with pain. Like one from whom people hide their faces He was despised, and we held Him in low esteem. ⁴Surely, He took up our pain and bore our suffering, yet we considered Him punished by God, stricken by Him, and afflicted."

⁵"But He was pierced for our transgressions, He was crushed for our iniquities; the punishment that brought us peace was on Him, and by His wounds we are healed. ⁶We all, like sheep, have gone astray, each of us has turned to our own way; and the Lord has laid on him the iniquity of us all."

⁷"He was oppressed and afflicted, yet He did not open His mouth; He was led like a lamb to the slaughter, and as a sheep before its shearers is silent, so He did not open His mouth. ⁸By oppression and judgment He was taken away. Yet who of His generation protested? For he was cut off from the land of the living; for the transgression of my people he was punished."

⁹ "He was assigned a grave with the wicked, and with the rich in His death, though He had done no violence, nor was any deceit in His mouth. ¹⁰Yet it was the Lord's will to crush Him and cause Him to suffer, and though the Lord makes His life an offering for sin, He will see His offspring and prolong His days, and the will of the Lord will prosper in His hand."

¹¹"After He has suffered, He will see the light of life, and be satisfied; by His knowledge my righteous servant will justify many, and He will bear their iniquities. ¹²Therefore I will give Him a portion among the great, and He will divide the spoils with the strong, because He poured out His life unto death, and was numbered with the transgressors. For He bore the sin of many, and made intercession for the transgressors."

The above Scripture was written about 700 years before the birth of Jesus. This Scripture is a part of the Old Testament which the Jewish people to this day still go by. Because the book of Isaiah is in their Bible, which is known as "The Torah." That Scripture from the Prophet Isaiah, has been the most effective Scripture and prophecy, to get those who believe in Judaism to believe in Jesus Christ being the Savior of the world. In "The Torah," He was predicted to be born and free their people. It certainly sounds like it describes what Jesus did for you and me, along with every other human being that inhabits planet earth. What do you think?

Every race has an entry fee. If you're running a Marathon or a triathlon, you're going to have to pay the price, to be allowed entry into the race.

Jesus paid for all our entry fees, with His own blood. Have you ever donated blood before? I'm ashamed to say that I have never donated blood before. I'm terrified of needles. Just the sight of seeing someone else getting a shot, makes me feel sick in the stomach. I have, however, given blood samples for, the purpose of getting, life insurance. In our world, it's a very respectable and noble thing to donate blood. You're saving someone's life by donating blood.

I remember when I was 18 years old. I saw an ad in the newspaper that said, "If you have a radio voice, we'd like to hire you." My whole life growing up, I always wanted to be on the radio. I would hide myself on the floor, of the front passenger's seat, of my dad's 1973 Ford Mustang. It was my little recording studio. I was extremely shy, and didn't want anyone to hear me. I would pretend that I had my own radio show, and would do all the voices of my guests who were singers. I had an old tape recorder that took "D" batteries. It blows my mind how far we've come along with technology. Now I have A full blown recording studio on my iPhone, and instead of using a typewriter to write this book, I'm typing it all out on my iPad Pro, with a 13-inch screen. The keyboard is folded up, and magnetically connected to the iPad cover. It's amazing how much we can achieve with technology. If only they could come up with a better way for drawing blood. Getting back to seeing the ad for people with a radio voice … I ended up applying for the position, and during the interview, I was told I would be reading radio commercials over the phone for local businesses all over the country, and that the radio commercial would be read to the small business owners, to get them to sponsor different campaigns, such as blood drives and missing children campaigns. It was a way for different radio stations to fill dead air space at their radio stations.

I would call up the different businesses and tell them that I had prepared a short radio commercial for their business, and would tell them that I'd like to read it to them. I won't go over what it said, but the main radio spot was meant to tug on the heart strings of people to donate blood generously. I accepted the position, and was very effective in getting businesses to sign up for the ad, and then one of the radio personalities, at the station, would record the spot for the business as the sponsor. My point here, is that people, especially here in the United States, know what a big deal it is to donate blood, so we can save peoples' lives when they need a blood transfusion. In my opinion, giving someone your blood, is the most important thing you can give them, other than donating your kidney or another organ.

With all of that said, I want you to think about what Jesus did for you and me. He not only donated His blood, but He sacrificed His body and His own life, by enduring a humiliating death on a cross. Sometimes in my own life, that doesn't seem like that big of a deal to me. I think it's because I wasn't there to see Him get crucified, and I didn't see Him getting whipped and beaten as the flesh on his back was torn to shreds. His face was punched so badly that it looked unrecognizable. But every time I watch a movie, like "The Passion of The Christ," or some other movie about Jesus that depicted the crucifixion, and the moments leading up to it, I am reminded of how big the price He paid for us was. And even in my own mind, as I see it in a movie, or try to imagine what it must have been like for Him to decide to do that for you and me, I still know that my gratitude and appreciation is not nearly enough. But I do think about, if I had to decide whether, or not to make that sacrifice, not by being forced to do it, but by doing it out of love and choice. He didn't have to go through what He went through. He chose to do it. You and I can have a better understanding and appreciation for what He did for us if we will take the time to think about the details of what He willingly went through for us to be forgiven.

The Eating and Training Plan He Puts His Players On

1 Timothy 4:8 *"For physical training is of some value, but Godliness has value for all things, holding promise for both the present life and the life to come."*

Daniel 1:11-15

[11] Daniel then said to the guard whom the chief official had appointed over Daniel, Hananiah, Mishael and Azariah, [12] "Please test your servants for ten days: Give us nothing but vegetables to eat and water to drink. [13] Then compare our appearance with that of the young men who eat the royal food, and treat your servants in accordance with what you see." [14] So he agreed to this and tested them for ten days.

[15] At the end of the ten days they looked healthier and better nourished than any of the young men who ate the royal food. [16] So the guard took away their choice food and the wine they were to drink and gave them vegetables instead.

The above two Scriptures blew me away when I first read them over 20 years ago. Since becoming a Christian, I have always been the kind of guy who wants to look my best, and obey the Scripture where God says to take care of your body because it's a holy temple that His Holy Spirit lives in. But even more so, I look at my body as a vessel. The vehicle, I have been given, by God to get to where He wants me to go. If I were to compare my body to a car, I would say that the physical training would be the body of the car. The engine would be the internal part that we don't see but, yet it's what gets the car to move, and provides all the horse power. Which, of course is what determines how fast you get there and how reliable the car is from breaking down on the side of the road. I've had many cars over the course of my life. I'm a big car guy who loves exotic looking cars. Usually foreign cars. But they tend to break down often, and when they do, it's very expensive to fix them. It's just like our physical bodies. The outward part of our body is like the body of a car. The interior of a car is still the visible outward features, that people see when driving in the car. But the engine is like the heart and soul of our bodies. You need to take care of what's inside, or the car body is useless.

Working out to me is very important. If I don't work out, I usually don't feel my best. When I combine working out with eating right, I'm feeling extra good. But when I'm getting into "His Game Changing Playbook," and praying to God for guidance and strength, I'm unstoppable, unless God decides to stop me. As 1 Timothy 4:8 says, *"physical training has some value, but Godliness has value for all things, holding promise for both the present life and the life to come."* The question I have for you is, what kind of fuel are you putting in your car? Are you putting in the cheapest, or most expensive gas? How about the oil? Are you changing it on a regular basis? What about the air filter and spark plugs? How about the recommended scheduled maintenance? What about the tires? Are you rotating them and changing them when they need to be changed? Are you starting to see my point? Just like a car that breaks down because it wasn't well maintained, our bodies breakdown and get diseases. And, in order, to get our bodies fixed, we sometimes end up in the hospital with hundreds of thousands of dollars, that are owed on medical bills, that can drive us to bankruptcy, or even worse, a breakdown in our physical, mental, emotional, and spiritual health. On a car, the most expensive thing to fix, would most likely be the engine. But even replacing the engine could only end up costing you 3 to 5 thousand dollars installed, if you found one used. But your body is the vessel that you rely on to take you where you want to go, and where Jesus wants you to go, to do His will.

Another point to consider when you're being a fisher of people, is setting the example to others, that you're reaching out to. What do you think their opinion of you is when they meet you? Do they look at you and think you're in great physical shape? As the Scripture says, physical training is of some value. I think some of that value would be in your visual testimony, as to how well disciplined you are as a Christian when it comes to your eating habits and physical discipline. So, if you're not in great physical shape right now, then you are most likely giving your body the wrong fuel, and not properly maintaining it. My cousin has been in management for many health clubs throughout the years. He said something that I'll never forget, when it comes to being in shape. He said, "Round is a shape, but it's not the shape you want to be in." I thought it was hilarious when he said it, but at the same time, I felt a bit sad, knowing how easy it is to get into that shape. Most of my life I have struggled with the battle of the cheeseburger, or the battle of the burrito. However, my biggest food battle has been the battle of the buffet. It's tough, to say the least about holding back from eating the delicious foods we want to eat. But it really is the equivalent of pouring sugar into your car's gas tank. It may not cause your car to break down instantly, but it will break down ... it's just a matter of time.

TO EAT OR NOT TO EAT THAT IS THE QUESTION

Daniel 1:12-15 talks about how Daniel and his 3 friends wanted to stay away from the Kings food and only eat vegetables and drink water. I for one have not made the move to being a complete vegetarian or vegan. But most of the time I stay away from eating meat because of the higher saturated fat content and the higher acidity found in meat. Romans 14:2 throws a bit of a monkey wrench into the eat only vegetables philosophy...or does it?

> Romans 14:2 *"One person's faith allows them to eat anything, but another, whose faith is weak, eats only vegetables."*

I have someone in my family who doesn't eat any meat at all. But that doesn't make them wrong. It's simply a matter of getting in the best spiritual and physical shape you can possibly be in. We all should strive to be the best we can be, because we're all in the starting line-up. And we want to run the best race we can possibly run. If the eating plan you're currently on, isn't helping you to look how you want to look, or feel how you want to feel, then it's time for a change. I highly recommend breaking the current eating plan you may be on, and replacing it with a 10-day fast, that includes only vegetables and water. It will jump start you into getting into great shape. I found that after going 10 days of eating only water and vegetables, I didn't want to go back to the buffet. If it worked for Daniel and his friends, it will work for you and me. It's

Jesus' strategic eating plan, to get all His players back into the best shape they can be in. You can look at it like an athlete who gets fat during the off season, but once spring training starts up, it's time to put the Doritos and pizza down, and start picking up some celery sticks.

HE WANTS YOU TO TURN YOUR TESTS INTO YOUR TESTIMONY

Have you ever wondered why you've had so many challenges, or testing times of your faith during your life? I know I've had many tests and challenges in my short 47 years of life on this planet. But no matter what I've ever gone through, I always try to look at all the good things in my life, during the testing times. I could write a whole book, just based on all the things that I think weren't fair in my life. Things that I didn't understand why God let me go through. But one of the ways I chose to look at those tests, was for me to realize, that those things I went through didn't happen to me, they happened for me. Every time I felt like I went through a setback, it was really a set up. A set up for what though? It was a set up for me to give my testimony to people I was trying to catch for "Team Jesus." So, let me ask you a question. How can you share the great things God has done in your life, during the difficult and dark times, if you've never had to go through any difficult times? You need to be tested, and able to see, if you've improved in your faith and wisdom. It's never fun to feel like you're a piece of bacon frying in the frying pan. The heat can get hot in life, and you can easily feel like you're shriveling up, and getting burnt. But the fact is, there's no avoiding these tests.

Just thinking about the times I've been able, to share with others about the very challenging times I had to go through in life, has made me feel grateful that I not only passed many of those tests, but that I came out even stronger. Plus, I've been able, to tell others that if God pulled me through that situation, and if I'm here to share this testimony with them, they can do the same. They can pull through their marriage, no matter how bad it is. Even if their spouse decides to quit on their marriage, I can tell them from my own personal experience, that God still has a great plan for them. I can share with them how I persevered through losing my father, grandma, and other losses in my life. Anything tough that I've ever had to deal with since becoming a Christian, Jesus has been right there with me, through thick and thin. Even when the finances were so low that I didn't know how I was going to get money for food to feed my family, He always provided in each, and every situation, through His people, along with His divine intervention. But you need to be ready to pass those tests. You need to exercise your faith, and listen to "The Coach."

If you're willing to do that, your comeback is guaranteed!!

You Are a Player Coach

Most motivational speakers, or success coaches, have assistant coaches. Some of the biggest success coaches, hire other success coaches, to work directly for them, and train them to teach their clients, exactly what's written in their bestselling books and seminars. Why would Jesus do things any differently? He's "The One" who created it all. He's "The One" who gave the wisdom to any success coach who has ever lived whether that coach knows it or not. To believe that all the wisdom that exists in this world, was created by a Big Bang, takes a lot of faith. I've read thousands of books, and listened to more motivational coaching programs than I can remember, over the last 25 years. With that said, most of the time I did exactly what the success coach, or motivational speaker said I should do, and it didn't work. And I'm not just saying that. I really did do it exactly the way they said. But I was always told that if it didn't work, it would be because of my limiting beliefs or subconscious beliefs. It would be self-sabotage.

That was the main truth, from most all the programs and books that I read. Jesus says that we must have faith, and without faith, it's impossible to please Him. He also said that we shouldn't expect to receive anything, unless we have faith. So, if you're being coached by Jesus, you need to understand the way He operates. He wants us to teach others what He has taught us. If we're going to teach others to succeed, then you and I can only teach what the coach teaches. The best way to do that, is to share with them, the best success book ever written, "The Bible." Before I became saved, I used to live my life by whatever motivational speakers' book I was reading at the time. After reading "The Bible," my whole world changed for the better. I understood where all wisdom came from. I could no longer deny that there was one book that gave us all the wisdom that's written in all the other success books. Any wisdom written in any other success or coaching book "that works," can be directly traced back to the Bible. Or as I like to refer to it as, "His Game Changing Playbook for Your Comeback!" Are you putting it to good use?

When You Believe, You Receive, But When You Doubt, You Go Without

Matthew 13:58 *"And He did not do many miracles there because of their lack of faith."*

I love that Scripture!! Because it clearly says that Jesus chose to not do many miracles because of their lack of faith. It's not that Jesus couldn't have performed more miracles if He wanted to. I believe He could have performed as many as He wanted to. But when someone designs a key to unlock a door, they want you to use the key. Breaking in or sneaking through the window isn't the way it's supposed to be. Jesus wants us to use the key that unlocks the door to all of God's best for our lives. Faith is the key that unlocks it all. As hard as it may be, to have faith in many situations or circumstances in our lives, we must understand that we hold an invisible key that works exactly like a physical key. Without the key, you're not getting into the locked door. Faith is a spiritual key. It's like having special mind powers to get what we want.

Hopefully you were fortunate enough to be raised by parents, who did nice things for you. If you did, then maybe you can remember times as a kid, when you would ask your parents for something you really wanted, and you believed wholeheartedly that not only would your parent or parents do or buy for you whatever it was that you were asking them for. Most likely you believed that they were fully able to do it. I know as a father, I love being able to do things for my kids. It's such a great feeling to know that my kids were being good kids, and that whatever they asked me for, I felt happy to give it to them. But if they came up to me, and asked me for something, and said, "I want you to do this for me, but I don't' believe you can do it for me." Or what if they told me that they think I'm a deadbeat dad, who never buys them anything, and only cares about myself? Now that would really hurt my feelings. So, what am I getting at here? I'm trying to help you to understand, that Jesus wants to know that He's believed in. That's what makes Him WANT to give us what we desire, as long, as it's something that's going to help us, and not hurt us. As a player coach for "Team Jesus", we need to understand His heart, for wanting to do good things for us. We need to believe what He says, and do it.

As a father, my kids know that they need to do what I tell them to do, and that they need to have faith in me, or my feelings are hurt. I try to do whatever I tell them that I'm going to do, so that they will continue to have faith in me. Of course, if I didn't do what I told them I would do, I would fully expect them to lose faith in me. That's why kids growing up, have a hard time believing in God being someone they can trust and believe in. The only example they have had in their lives, was someone who didn't come through, with what they asked for. Someone who meant well, but didn't understand how important it was, to keep their word to their kids. I always tell my kids that I'm only human, and that I'm always trying my best. And that's the best gift we can give to anyone in our lives.

> 2 Corinthians 1:20 *"For no matter how many promises God has made, they are "Yes" in Christ. And so, through Him the "Amen" is spoken by us to the glory of God."*

What I love most about that Scripture, is that God keeps His promises in Jesus' Name. You and I can trust 100% that if we persist in having faith, we will receive whatever we ask for, as long, as it's something that will help us, and not hurt us. If your kid wanted you to buy them a pet Boa Constrictor snake, that could escape the aquarium or cage, and possibly kill them, would you buy it for them? Probably not. I believe it's the same exact thing when it comes to whether or not Jesus answers our prayers.

The 2-Minute Warning

Have you ever watched any sporting event, where there was only a couple of minutes left on the game clock? Maybe it was a baseball game and it was the bottom of the ninth, and the team up to bat was down by 5 runs, and this was their last chance to win. Maybe it was a basketball or soccer game. Whatever game it was, the teams competing knew that their time to win was running out. I'll use the example of football, because there's a 2-minute warning, before the first half ends, and then at the end of the fourth quarter. All of a sudden, the two-minute warning hits, and the losing team suddenly comes to life, and lays it all on the line. If they're tired, they get the wind back in their sails. If they're injured, they suddenly ignore the pain, and they play all out. If the losing team has spent most of the game running the ball, they all, of a sudden decide to start throwing deep to score a quick touchdown. They no longer play it safe, and they no longer waste any more time on the game clock. They lay it all on the line. They no longer worry about failure, or looking stupid while their trying to win. They just go for it. It's extremely exciting to watch. I mentioned earlier about the New England Patriots amazing comeback against the Atlanta Falcons in the Super Bowl. If you haven't seen it, I recommend you go on YouTube and, at least, watch the highlights of the game.

The fork was stuck in the pig. The fat lady had sung and it was over! But there were two key people involved who made any Patriot fan, or anyone who knew about the Patriots' team, hold off on giving them their last rites. The Patriots had a proven future hall of fame quarterback in

Tom Brady. They also had a future hall of fame coach, in Bill Belichick. And when you have 2 people on a team like that, you know what they have done in the past for many seasons. So, the opposing team knows what they're capable of. When the 2-minute warning hit, the Patriots had the momentum, and you knew that it was possible for them to pull off perhaps the greatest football comeback of all time. You had faith in them as a team, because you knew who was on the team, and who was leading it. You knew the plays that would be called, would most likely be executed properly. You also knew that they would be great plays. The timing was also right. Tom Brady had an axe to grind, with the commissioner of the NFL, for imposing the suspension on him for "Deflate Gate." If you're not familiar with the scandal, then here's what allegedly happened. Tom was accused of having the footballs deflated below the leagues acceptable limit for super bowl play. Tom and his lawyers fought the claims and suspension, until the very end. But he unsuccessfully fought the accusations, and it ended up tarnishing his reputation and pride.

Jesus was falsely accused as well. He had an axe to grind with the false accuser of His people. He was driven to His victorious comeback, by showing the Head coach of "The Hell City Demons," that victory would still be His and His players, in-spite of the false accusations and lies, that were said about Him. Don't get me wrong. I'm not saying that I know whether, or not Tom Brady was guilty of having the balls deflated to get a competitive advantage. But I can tell you, that the proof is always in the pudding. It didn't look like Tom Brady needed deflated balls to pull off one of, or perhaps even the greatest comeback in sporting event history.

How Much Time Is Left on Your Game Clock?

I was just out to lunch a few days ago to celebrate my belated 47th birthday, with some of my in-laws. I've been very blessed with great in-laws. My mother in-law and father in-law are great Christians. During our lunch, I was discussing my age with my father in-law, and told him that I couldn't believe I was already 47. I told him that when I was a teenager, I used to look at 47-year old's as really, old. I would call them old farts. I mentioned to my father in-law how people my age, can suddenly drop dead of a heart attack. I told him that when you're my age, you just don't know how many years you have left to live. He responded with, "When you get to be my age, you don't wonder how many years you have left, you wonder how many days you have left." I thought about what he said all throughout the rest of the day. I realized, that he's well aware of the 2-minute warning in his life. His statement also made me think that perhaps we might even be in the 2-second warning of our lives. You just never know how much time is left on your game clock.

In the two-minute warning, things get serious. The past doesn't matter. The only thing that matters is the present moment. Where are you at, in your life right now? Are you in the 2-minute warning of your life? The correct answer to that question, is that you or I don't know. Only God knows how much time is left on our game clock. I remember being 12 years old, and watching a documentary on Michael Landon. He's the guy who was mostly known for the role he played, as the dad on Little House on The Prairie. He also played the role of "Little Joe Cartwright" on the 70's tv show called Bonanza. His final tv series was "Highway to Heaven." He was doing a tv interview, because he had been diagnosed with terminal pancreas and liver cancer. He was told he only had a month or so left to live, according to the doctors. And I'll never forget what he said during the interview he had. It looked like just about every major news outlet at the time was in attendance. He was asked by one of the reporters, what advice he would give to anyone, about how to live their life, now that he's been given this news from the doctor? What he said, was the best advice anyone could ever receive, regarding how to live. I've tried to remember this, whenever I felt I was taking life for granted. He said, "If only someone would tell us that on the day we're born we're already dying. So, we would live our lives to the fullest and not waste it." I'm paraphrasing, so please don't quote me. He also said to the reporters interviewing him, "Live every minute guys."

That's how we can live our life like the 2-minute warning. That's what we must remember, when we say we're going to do something next year, next week or even tomorrow. We need to realize that the game clock is ticking, and that the time could be up at any second. Sometimes I get indigestion, or some little discomfort in my chest, and I automatically start thinking, "Maybe it's my heart. Hopefully I don't have a heart attack." And I don't try to focus in on that thought, because I know that our thoughts are seeds, that will grow into fruition if we keep watering and fertilizing them. But it's important for us to realize, that we are not even guaranteed to be here, a second from now.

THOUGHTS ARE SEEDS

THE PARABLE OF THE SOWER

Matthew 13:1-9

> *¹That same day Jesus went out of the house and sat by the lake. ²Such large crowds gathered around him that he got into a boat and sat in it, while all the people stood on the shore. ³Then he told them many things in parables, saying: "A farmer went out to sow his seed. ⁴As he was scattering the seed, some fell along the path, and the birds came and ate it up. ⁵Some fell on rocky places, where it did not have much soil. It sprang up quickly, because the soil was shallow. ⁶But when the sun came up, the plants were scorched, and they withered because they had no root. ⁷Other seed fell among thorns, which grew up and choked the plants. ⁸Still other seed fell on good soil, where it produced a crop—a hundred, sixty or thirty times what was sown. ⁹Whoever has ears, let them hear."*

As I mentioned earlier, thoughts are seeds. Whatever you think about, and continue to water and fertilize, will become your reality. As you can see in the above parable that Jesus told, it's all about the seed and the soil. The soil of this world is dirt. The soil of the spiritual realm is your heart, soul, and mind. The mind is the gatekeeper to the heart and soul. The eyes are a window into the mind. The ears are also an entry way into the mind by what you allow them to hear. Whatever seeds of thought you allow to be planted into your mind, is exactly what starts to take root, and will eventually be full grown, and multiply into your life. Jesus doesn't want you to focus on defeat. He wants you to focus in on victory. We've all heard the saying of, "Whether you think you can, or think you can't, either way you're right." That's so true. If you don't think you can do something, then you won't be willing to take the necessary action to even try. If you're a salesman, and you're trying to sell something that you don't believe in, or you think costs too much, then you won't even try to sell it, because you yourself wouldn't be willing to buy it. And that's where the key is. You need to sell yourself on something, or you won't do it. I have been in sales for most of my adult life, and I always had to be sold on whatever I was trying to sell. Otherwise, I didn't want to approach others about buying it. It felt more like scamming someone, rather than helping them. Even before I became a Christian, I knew it wasn't right in good conscience, to sell something you didn't believe in. Those thoughts of disbelief, translated into bad sales. But on the flip-side, if I believed in something or someone, I was always able to sell it, and to sell a lot of it. Looking back at my life, I now understand, that every single time I didn't believe in something or someone, it was never a good situation. If I don't believe in something, that means I'm having doubt. We need to make sure that we don't end up planting seeds of doubt. When that seed of doubt is consistently watered, it grows into failure.

You get whatever seed you plant. We all understand in the physical realm, that if we plant a corn seed, we're going to harvest corn. Of course, the same is true, for any other seed. Each seed will produce what you expect it to produce. As I said before, our thoughts are seeds, and there is absolutely no difference between our thought seeds, and the physical seeds of this world. Just like in the physical world, when we water the seed, and pull the weeds out of the garden, to protect what we want to grow. In the garden of our mind, we must make sure that we don't allow the weeds to take over. Anything you could possibly want, if it's according to Gods will, you can get it, if you continue to have the thoughts that He can do anything, if you ask Him. But you must have faith in Him that He's able to do it. Continuous faith equals continuous watering of the seed. We must choose to believe that the Bible is 100% true, and incorruptible by man. We must believe that what it says, can, and will be used in your life, if you will simply continue to water those thought seeds. God will bless your thoughts, when they're combined with faith in Him, and His promises, that are in "His Game Changing Playbook for Your Comeback."

How to Stop Sleeping the Time Off Your Game Clock

Have you ever felt like not doing something to the point that you're willing to clean up the house or garage instead of doing what you're putting off? In my case, cleaning up dog poop seemed like a better alternative to going to a job I hated. That's how I felt every day of the work week, until I decided to follow my dreams wholeheartedly. I used to wake up feeling discouraged, and completely not excited to start the day, because I was bored of the same routine. I was sick and tired of doing what I knew I couldn't stand doing. I knew that I wanted to make a change in my life, but I was too afraid to do it. But I found a way to do it even though I just didn't want to. I started each day extra early. And when I say early, I'm talking about 4:30 am wake up time. I usually slept in until between 7:30 to 8:00 am … it all depended on how discouraged I felt on that particular morning. If I woke up early in the past for some reason, such as the dogs barking, or having to go to the bathroom, I would lay in bed until I could fall back asleep. Of course, when I woke up, I would have my coffee, and then procrastinate by going on YouTube, or checking out the news sites. And then I would read something in the Bible, and then a positive book of some sort. And since I'm self-employed, I had all the time and freedom in the world. But I was wasting it by procrastinating. The problem I had was that my primary source of income, involved me doing something that didn't challenge me, and didn't make my soul come alive, with the thought of doing it. My main dream in life has always been to do music. I sing, write songs, perform live, and love the recording process in the studio.

I figured out that as a kid, the only times I would wake up at 4:30 am in the morning, was when it was Christmas, Easter, or my Birthday. And the reason I would wake up early was because I was extremely excited about that day. I absolutely loved getting gifts and eating candy. But then again, what kid doesn't? So, I realized that if I could start each day knowing the night before, that I was going to be able to wake up and be able to make my coffee, and then start doing what I loved, I would be motivated to get out of bed right away. If you have a full-time job, and work the 9 to 5 office thing, then this will still work for you. If your passion is music, art, or even watching movies. You could set your alarm clock for 4:30am, 5:00am, or whatever time you're willing to get up, and start your morning routine. We all have a routine. But is your routine helping you to live your dreams? If the answer is no, then it's time to change it. I was talking to one of my sons, on the way to dropping him off at school, about how much he hated going to school, because he felt that it was useless stuff he was learning. He felt that it was taking too many hours away from what he really wanted to do, which is making Anime Art, and playing video games, along with eating delicious food and snacks. I had already been into my new life changing routine for a few months, and was able to share with him, my new plan that I learned from, "His Game Changing Play Book."

> Proverbs 20:13 *"Do not love sleep or you will grow poor; stay awake and you will have food to spare."*

The reason I love that Scripture so much, is because being poor, is not just about money. Being poor, could be in any area of our lives. We are used to thinking that being poor is only about money. My grandma used to tell me all the time when I was growing up, that as-long-as I have my health, I have everything. She was so right. I always knew that she meant having our health, in addition to having Jesus in our lives. We can also be rich in passion. When you have your health and you wake up with passion every morning, because you know that you're going to do what you love, that makes you come alive. That makes you rich.

You Gotta Have a Dream

I mentioned to you before about my dad telling me one time when he was really struggling with his drinking addiction that he had been at the tail end of a 2-week plus drinking binge, and he wasn't doing very well to say the least. He always liked to talk when he was drinking. He was very lonely, and very sad, most of the time when he was in that state. But when he was drinking, he was usually very truthful about his feelings and his thoughts. When he was drunk, it was the only time he would say, "I love you" to me or my brothers. One time, in particular, as he broke down and cried, he told me that he doesn't feel like he has a reason to live anymore. He said that he's lost all his dreams. I couldn't help but to break down and cry with him. I believe I was about 18 at the time, and I didn't understand what he was really talking about, because at that particular time in my life, I was overflowing with dreams. Everything was possible for me. I just had to figure out exactly what I wanted, and how to do it. I pretty much knew at that time that I wanted to make it big as a singer and songwriter.

Looking back now, at the age of 47, I know exactly what my dad was saying. As my face has aged, and the grey hair has shown up, I know he was well-aware that the clock was running out on his life and dreams. It wasn't that he didn't have any dreams left. It was that he didn't think he had enough time to achieve them. He was choking on all the past regrets of his life. He wasn't upset about the things he did in his life. He was more upset about the things he didn't do in his life. He never really went for any of his dreams, except for when he was on his way to making it to the big leagues as a baseball pitcher. And then as I told you earlier, his dreams came crashing down when he fell several floors, almost to his death, from that nearly fatal elevator accident. I'm going to ask you a question, and I want you to be completely honest with yourself. Ok? Is there anything in your life that you have always dreamed of doing or becoming, but you told yourself that you didn't have the talent, money, or time to make it happen? Hopefully, the answer is no. Hopefully, you're living or going after all your dreams to the fullest, as you're reading this book. But if the answer is "yes," and there's a dream you felt like you should've gone for, then I'm here to tell you, that it's not too late. It's only, too late if you decide it's too late. I'm here to tell you that I have gone after every dream that I've ever had up to this point in my life, because I realize how painful regret can be. I thank God that He let me understand that pain through the conversation I had with my dad, on that tearful day. Don't let yourself choke on regret. Don't accept any lies from the opposing team, that it's too late. It's not too late! You have everything, and everyone you need, to make it happen. Everything you need can be found in "His Game Changing Playbook." The everyone you need is found in God the Father, God the Son, and God the Holy Spirit.

How to Get Your Momentum Back

> Romans 7:15 *"I do not understand what I do. For what I want to do I do not do, but what I hate I do."*

I brought up earlier about doing things even if you don't feel like it. But let's talk about doing things that we know we don't want to do. The Scripture above talks about doing what you hate to do. Doing what you hate to do is doing anything you know you shouldn't do, but you do it anyway, even if you get a bunch of pleasure out of doing it. Your conscience suffers by doing what you know you shouldn't do because you know you shouldn't be doing it. But you do it anyway. And then the pattern of losing respect and faith in yourself, continues. But there's a way to stop doing what you hate, and to start doing what you know you should do. The solution is to just do it. Yep! Just like the Nike slogan says, "It's as simple as that." But with one added ingredient. You have "The Greatest Coach of All Time" coaching you. You also have unlimited access to His "Holy Spirit" and "His Game Changing Playbook for Your Comeback."

The reason you need to do, what you don't feel like doing, is because every journey begins with the first step. And the first step is always the hardest step to take. I have struggled with my weight since the age of 25. When my first son was on the way, I became very discouraged because I thought that my musical dreams were dead. I wasn't planning on being a father at that time in my life, and when reality had set in that I may have blown my chance to move to Nashville, Tennessee, or Music City USA as some call it, I decided to start getting more into my drug of choice at the time, which was fattening and delicious foods. I started inhaling pizza rolls and ice cream like a vacuum cleaner. I got extremely fat. I knew that at some point, I would need to eat right, and start working out again, but I couldn't seem to get myself to take the first step. Finally, I was told about an amazing book called "Body for Life," which was written by a great guy named Bill Phillips. The book was life changing, because after reading it, I was excited to take that first step. The best part about doing the "Body for Life" plan, or challenge, was that I would get 1 day a week to not exercise, and to eat anything I wanted for the entire day. I knew that if I was allowed, to take 1 day a week to be a glutton, I could push through 6 days of eating extremely healthy. So, I would take that free day literally, and I would have my pizza in the oven, and be ready to take it out as soon as the clock hit 12 Midnight. That was technically when my free day began.

Looking back now, it makes me laugh, that I was so obsessed with food. I would have my ice cream and pie waiting to be devoured, as soon as I was finished eating the entire pizza. I was so excited to be a glutton at the time. But now I don't look at my eating that way, I just try to always eat healthy, and take a cheat meal, once or twice a week. I now realize that momentum gets stronger or it gets weaker. Momentum either moves towards winning or losing, success or failure. Today my life is different. When I know there's something I need to do, I just begin to do it, and I find that after taking the first step, the second step gets easier than the first, and then the 3rd step gets easier as well. If I get discouraged, and fall off the wagon, I take the first step again, towards my goal or objective, and the same pattern repeats in a positive direction. The goal isn't to be perfect. The goal is to be the best me, that I can be. Are you being the best version of you? If not, then take the step right now to be that person you have always wanted to be. Be the person, that you have always believed, deep down in your soul, that you could be.

You Haven't Got a Prayer

Matthew 6:5-8

> *⁵"And when you pray, do not be like the hypocrites, for they love to pray standing in the synagogues and on the street corners to be seen by others. Truly I tell you, they have received their reward in full. ⁶But when you pray, go into your room, close the door, and pray to your Father, who is unseen. Then your Father, who sees what is done in secret, will reward you. ⁷And when you pray, do not keep on babbling like pagans, for they think they will be heard because of their many words. ⁸Do not be like them, for your Father knows what you need before you ask him."*

When it comes to winning, losing, or getting what we want in life, one of the most popular sayings I've ever heard was, "You haven't got a prayer." I'll never forget this one time I went out to lunch with a few different friends from church. We had just received our food from the waitress, and I was starving. My big juicy bacon cheeseburger was just begging me to eat it. One of my friends ended up being the one to say a prayer of gratitude for our food. I'll never forget it as-long-as I live, because when this friend of ours prayed, his prayer must have lasted about 5 minutes. There were a couple of girls from the church, who were very outspoken, and knew this mutual friend of ours very well. So, as we were all trying not to salivate over our plates, this friend of ours kept praying and praying, until one of the young ladies interrupted his prayer and said, "Don't be trying to have your quiet time here." It was so funny, that nearly 20 years later it still cracks me up. It reminds me of the Scripture above. This guy was a great guy, but it seemed like he truly enjoyed praying in front of others. It was almost the equivalent of someone standing up and doing a freestyle rap, except in the form of a prayer. But this guy's reaction was priceless. After she said that, he instantly stopped his prayer and said, "In Jesus's name, Amen." Right after he said "amen," we all started inhaling our food.

That experience really showed me that praying isn't something we should try to impress others with. Praying isn't something we should look at as something we're good at. When I pray, I pray to God in Jesus' name, as I would speak to my earthly father. I try to be myself, and be honest with God. After all, He made us, and can read our hearts and minds. So, it's kind of ridiculous to try and be fake with Him. The only way to be with Him, is GENUINE. It's time to stop trying to fool God, and time to be real with Him. We must rely on Him and trust Him as you're Father, who just happens to be in Heaven, but at the same time He's present with you at this very moment. He's everywhere at all times. And even though you and I can't understand how He can do that, we need to acknowledge to ourselves, that it's ok to not understand everything right now. Even if you don't understand everything, you can understand the most basic way as a Christian to win in life. If you can be real with God, and pray to Him, or say to Him whatever's on your heart and mind, and if you're willing to take off the mask, and be real with Him, then you will truly have a prayer!!

How Many Times Should You Forgive Someone?

Matthew 6:15 *"But if you do not forgive others their sins, your Father will not forgive your sins."*

The Parable of the Unmerciful Servant

Matthew 18:21-35

> [21] *"Then Peter came to Jesus and asked, "Lord, how many times shall I forgive my brother or sister who sins against me? Up to seven times?*
>
> [22] *Jesus answered, "I tell you, not seven times, but seventy-seven times."*
>
> [23] *"Therefore, the Kingdom of Heaven is like a king who wanted to settle accounts with his servants.* [24] *As he began the settlement, a man who owed him ten thousand bags of gold was brought to him.* [25] *Since he was not able to pay, the master ordered that he and his wife and his children and all that he had be sold to repay the debt.*
>
> [26] *"At this the servant fell on his knees before him. 'Be patient with me,' he begged, 'and I will pay back everything.'*

²⁷ The servant's Master took pity on him, canceled the debt and let him go.

²⁸ "But when that servant went out, he found one of his fellow servants who owed him a hundred silver coins. He grabbed him and began to choke him. 'Pay back what you owe me!' he demanded.

²⁹ "His fellow servant fell to his knees and begged him, 'Be patient with me, and I will pay it back.'

³⁰ "But he refused. Instead, he went off and had the man thrown into prison until he could pay the debt. ³¹ When the other servants saw what had happened, they were outraged and went and told their master everything that had happened.

³² "Then the master called the servant in. 'You wicked servant,' he said, 'I canceled all that debt of yours because you begged me to. ³³ Shouldn't you have had mercy on your fellow servant just as I had on you?' ³⁴ In anger his master handed him over to the jailers to be tortured, until he should pay back all he owed.

³⁵ "This is how my heavenly Father will treat each of you unless you forgive your brother or sister from your heart."

The above parable is a bit long, but I wanted to include the whole parable so you could fully understand what Jesus thinks about any of his players who refuse to forgive someone who has sinned against them. If it seems like I'm repeating the subject of forgiveness in this book, it's because I am. It's the most important thing Jesus wants to teach us to put into practice as Christians, other than loving Him, and our neighbors. This topic is perhaps one of the most difficult areas of my life, and many other people's lives, when it comes to obeying our Coach. Does Jesus really mean "77" times? Or does he simply mean that we should always forgive the person not for their sake alone, but for the sake of our own well-being, and for the sake of obeying what Jesus says we need to do? After all, didn't Jesus die on the cross for you and I, as well as for the sins of the whole world to be forgiven, if anyone is willing to let go of their own unforgiveness?

I understand the parable of the unmerciful servant as Jesus letting you and I, know how wrong it is, and how hypocritical it is to receive forgiveness and to want forgiveness, only to deny others of the very same gift you have been given. I'm not trying to preach to anyone about anything that I'm not willing to do. As hard as it is to forgive others when they sin against us, we're not only helping them to heal, but we're also healing our own hurts, and healing our own emotional scars as well. Once we forgive someone, the pain and anguish we feel in our own souls, is gone. Because I know how good it feels to truly forgive someone from the heart, I would like you to have that same feeling. Every time I made the decision to forgive someone, the tears fell like rain, and it was as if the sun began to shine again after a thunderstorm.

As Jesus says in Matthew 6:15, I'll paraphrase, "If you don't forgive others, YOU WON'T BE FORGIVEN." That's reason enough to forgive others. Once I understood that, my whole world changed.

WE WIN BY LOSING

> Matthew 16:25 *"For whoever wants to save their life will lose it, but whoever loses their life for me will find it."*

The Scripture above comes straight out of Jesus' mouth. He's not telling us to physically die. He's telling us that we need to lose the current life we've been living, which is the life that we've become used to. It's the comfort zone life. We have our certain sins that we enjoy and hold dearly, but when Jesus is your Coach, He wants you to stop living your life the way you've been living it, and to start living it the way that He knows is best for you. And of course, He has a Playbook, that will tell you exactly how He wants you to live it. I remember when I knew that I couldn't put off losing my life of willing sin any longer. That sounds weird, doesn't it? To me, losing my life sounded very painful. But Jesus says the good news, is that by losing your life, you end up winning in life. He says that whoever loses their life for Him, will find their life. That's so deep, isn't it?

When I made my decision to lose my life, I was thinking about a movie that I loved growing up, called, "Lost Boys." It was such a cool movie. It was about these 2 brothers who moved to Santa Monica California, with their single Mom. While living there, the older brother met a big group of wild and reckless teenagers who had their own club. It turns out that they were all teenage vampires. They recruited the older brother into their group, by luring him in with a girl who was also a vampire in the group, that he was really digging. They peer pressured him into drinking some blood from a wine bottle, in front of the girl he was wanting to impress. So, he ended up drinking some of the blood. After drinking some of the blood, he slowly started turning into a vampire. He needed to wear sunglasses the very next day, because the sun, as we all know, doesn't mix with vampires. His younger brother started to notice some crazy things about the brother, who was showing signs of turning into a vampire. I won't ruin the movie for you, because if you haven't seen it yet, I highly recommend you do. Even though it's a movie from the 80's, you'll thoroughly enjoy it. So, the younger brother ends up calling these two teenage brothers, who were like the ghostbusters of vampires. They were called, "Edgar and Allen Frog" … The Frog brothers. They were hilarious. So, to make a long story short, I felt that losing my worldly life was a bit like becoming a vampire. But I had it all wrong. I thought that I was going to become some type of Jesus Freak. I thought that I needed to become one of those weird people who tried to force feed Jesus to you, by trying to cram a Bible down your throat. I didn't realize that being a Christian could be so cool. I had no idea that my life wasn't going to get weird or bad. But that it would become a life of peace, clarity & coolness.

I no longer worried about what I wanted to do with my life. I started thinking about what Jesus wanted to do with my life. I found out first hand, that Jesus wasn't lying, when He said that I would find my life by losing it for Him. It's a lot like jumping into a pool of freezing cold water. You are not wanting to jump in, because you know it's going to be very cold at first. But then you jump in, and the water wasn't as cold as you thought. And then the water temperature ends up feeling just right. I don't know where you're at spiritually as you're reading these words, but I can tell you that no matter where you're at with your walk with Jesus, sometimes you need to re-lose your life. My old life kept trying to find me. To this day it still tries to re-attach itself to me. But I look at it as a lizard sheds its skin. My old life has been shed and I am a new creation who has been born again. There's no reason for me to put the grave clothes back on. The old life I lived is gone, dead and buried.

Jesus Hangs Out with The Tailgaters

Luke 5:29-32

> *²⁹Then Levi held a great banquet for Jesus at his house, and a large crowd of tax collectors and others were eating with them. ³⁰But the Pharisees and the teachers of the law who belonged to their sect complained to his disciples, "Why do you eat and drink with tax collectors and sinners?"*
>
> *³¹Jesus answered them, "It is not the healthy who need a doctor, but the sick. ³²I have not come to call the righteous, but sinners to repentance."*

If you've ever been to a tailgate party, then you know there's a bunch of beer, food and people getting ready to celebrate victory. There's a bunch of Christians whom I've personally known throughout my life, who wouldn't want to hang out with people who are getting drunk and eating a bunch of unhealthy food. As a recovered Pharisee myself, I used to think that wasn't where I should hang out. But when I recovered, and understood that that's exactly where Jesus would be found if He were hanging out with us today, I realized that I needed to tailgate as well. The first step to recovering as a Pharisee, is to stop judging everyone as a sinful wretch. Even after we become Christians, we're still sinful wretches who are continuously in need of forgiveness. And we continually need to repent. It's a daily renewing that we go through in-order to be the best for our Coach. He paid the price for our sins. And He has allowed us to stay in the game, because of the daily forgiveness and grace that He gives to us. Think about it. How could anyone be a fisher of people if they're unwilling to hang out with the people who are not yet caught? You'd also be surprised to find some great Christian brothers and sisters at the tailgate party you attend. They just realized before you did, that Jesus wanted them to be there.

The reason I write and sing different types of songs, and not just 100% Christian songs, is because someone who's not yet a Christian, isn't going to be listening to Christian songs. But they will be listening to songs about a relationship, or songs about a party. You may disagree with my approach to being a fisher of people, but if I'm going to reach people through my songs, they're going to most likely, listen to one of my non-Christian songs, and then hopefully like the song enough to check out some of my other songs about Jesus. I used to be a holier than art thou Christian. The kind that would be looking at other people's sins, and not focusing in on my own. That was a very bad place for me to be in my Christian walk. Some Christians get extremely up-tight if they see another Christian drinking a beer. Some Christians think that the water that Jesus turned into wine, was only turned into grape juice, because grape juice didn't have any alcohol in it. I had to search out different Scriptures to find out what God's Word said about wine. I'm not condoning anyone to become a drunkard, but I'm going to share the following Scripture with you that talks about wine being good for health benefits. So, if you're currently in Alcoholics Anonymous, or Narcotics Anonymous, and you're wanting to use this Scripture to fall off the wagon and start being a wine addict, please don't justify doing that based on the following Scripture. I'm only trying to make a point, for any of our brothers and sisters in Christ, who believe that Jesus turned water into grape juice.

> 1 Timothy 5:23 *"Stop drinking only water, and use a little wine because of your stomach and your frequent illnesses."*

Use a little wine obviously means to drink a little wine. Notice how God's Word doesn't say to guzzle a bottle of wine. It merely says that drinking a little wine is good for your stomach and health. My goal in writing this once again, is to get you to no longer treat other Christians or Non-Christians, who drink a little wine or beer, like they have leprosy, or are to be judged as sinful wretches, because you think that anyone who drinks wine or alcohol is ungodly. For the record, I rarely drink any alcohol, and when I do, it's usually once every few years. I don't drink much, because it usually ends up making me sick. Now let's talk about the tax collectors and sinners that the Pharisees had a problem with. They didn't want Jesus to hang out with sinners, period. But isn't that arrogant and snobbish of them? Jesus simply says that He's there for the sick, because they're the ones who need a Doctor, to help them heal. The prescription Jesus has for them and us, is to stop sinning, because He knows that sin in our lives is like cancerous tumors in our bodies. He knows what's best for us. He knows that sin hurts us and kills our dreams, along with the plans He has for our lives. I know that I'm not the most, Godly Christian at times, and that I need Jesus to help me to overcome the sins that the enemy wants me to partake in daily. BUT I look to Jesus as my Coach, and he helps to remind me to follow His game plan which is His Bible and owner's manual for our lives. I challenge you to stop judging, and to start fishing for people in the pond where they're not caught yet.

He's Going to Help You Finish the Game

Philippians 1:3-6

> ³"I thank my God every time I remember you. ⁴In all my prayers for all of you, I always pray with joy ⁵because of your partnership in the gospel from the first day until now, ⁶being confident of this, that he who began a good work in you will carry it on to completion until the day of Christ Jesus."

Our teammates are praying for us. They're praying that we don't lose faith in our Coach. Jesus began a good work in us, but what is that good work? I think that good work, is what His playbook has done, to show us how to leave our life of sin, and ungodliness. He showed us how to win in life, and to live a life He can say He's proud of us for living. Just as you want to make your earthly parents proud, you should want to make your Heavenly Father proud. And what exactly is being referred to in that Scripture regarding the day of Christ Jesus? It's when Jesus is going to return and take all His people with Him to Heaven. It's known as the rapture.

1 Thessalonians 4:13-18

> ¹³"Brothers and sisters, we do not want you to be uninformed about those who sleep in death, so that you do not grieve like the rest of mankind, who have no hope. ¹⁴For

> we believe that Jesus died and rose again, and so we believe that God will bring with Jesus those who have fallen asleep in him. [15]According to the Lord's word, we tell you that we who are still alive, who are left until the coming of the Lord, will certainly not precede those who have fallen asleep. [16]For the Lord himself will come down from heaven, with a loud command, with the voice of the archangel and with the trumpet call of God, and the dead in Christ will rise first. [17]After that, we who are still alive and are left will be caught up together with them in the clouds to meet the Lord in the air. And so, we will be with the Lord forever. [18]Therefore encourage one another with these words."

As you can tell from reading this book, I'm really, big on showing you what the Bible says. I don't want you to take my word for it, I want you to take Gods Word for it. You could go up to 90% of the Christians, and ask them if they know what's going to happen when Jesus comes back, and most of them would say that they're not sure. It's going to be one heck of a day. The Scripture above, says that we're going to be gathered with Him, up in the clouds, and that we're not going to have to experience the physical earthly death if we're still alive when He comes back for us. I think we're currently in the 2- minute warning with regards to Jesus coming back. Perhaps you and I can avoid going through a physical death. That would be fine with me. I don't know about you, but I want to be one of the people gathered up in the clouds, who gets to avoid having to die. Dying doesn't sound like a fun experience to me. How about you? Are you ready for the day "The Coach" comes back? Are you living your life in His mercy and grace, and not thinking that you can earn it by your good works or deeds? Are you stuck in the old mentality of earning your salvation, because you can list off a bunch of good things that you do as a person? God says in His Word, that we all fall short of His glory, and all of us have sinned. If we all try to swim across the ocean, and none of us reach the shore, have any of us won? Not according to God. The goal was to swim across the ocean and to reach the shore. If none of us reached it, then we all, definitely, fell short.

WE ALL FALL SHORT

Romans 3:22-24

> *²²"This righteousness is given through faith in Jesus Christ to all who believe. There is no difference between Jew and Gentile, ²³for all have sinned and fall short of the glory of God, ²⁴and all are justified freely by his grace through the redemption that came by Christ Jesus."*

How do you like them apples? We all have sinned, and we all fall short of the glory of God. It's a level playing field. None of us can boast about being any better than each other. If everyone falls short of the finish line in a race, then who can say they won? It's just like the example I gave in the previous chapter about swimming across the ocean. The great news is that even though we all fall short, we all get to win, because Jesus makes us all winners, even though we all fall short of the finish line. It's by His grace that we get to win. And you get to win, IF you believe that He died for your sins, and that He is who He says He is. You win if you believe, that He can and will do, what He said he'd do for you, me, and the whole word. If you don't believe in Him, or what He says, you automatically lose. The only thing you're left with, is to say that nobody knows what's true, and that choosing not to believe anything, justifies you, and gives you the victory. As they say, "you've got to stand for something, or you'll fall for anything." Do you stand for the truth, or do you stand for indecisiveness, and anything goes? Either way, I don't judge you. But I'll pray for you, to take a stand for the truth, and to make a decision as to what you believe. I'll pray that you'll choose to have faith in Jesus. Because if you choose to not have faith in Jesus, then you're choosing to have faith in your decision to not have faith in Him. Perhaps you're putting your faith into Darwinism, or something else you believe. But the bottom-line is that you need to have faith in whatever it is that you choose to believe, because whatever you state as a fact, has to be believed as the truth.

The Earth, Sun, Moon, and Stars

> Isaiah 40:22 *"He sits enthroned above the circle of the earth, and its people are like grasshoppers. He stretches out the heavens like a canopy, and spreads them out like a tent to live in."*

Scholars have said that the book of Isaiah was written approximately 700 years BC, which means before Christ walked the earth. Isn't it amazing how Isaiah the prophet knew that the earth was a circle? And of course, a circle is the shape of a ball. So basically, we live on a big ball. The sun is a big ball of fire. And the moon is a ball that looks like Swiss cheese. The planet Saturn has a ring around it, that looks like one of those extra cool frisbees, that I played with when I was a kid. There's literally millions of stars in the sky, that we can see through the Hubble telescope. If we look up into the sky, we can see unlimited stars with our eyes.

I was talking to my son the other day about how the earth is a big ball suspended over nothingness. It's suspended in thin air. I asked him if he was impressed that this big ball that we live on, can stay suspended over nothingness with all of us humans, cars, buildings, and other things that are on planet earth. I also asked him how much he thought the earth weighed. And he brought to my attention, that all the cars and buildings, were made from everything that's already on the earth, so the weight of the earth really isn't increasing. But then I mentioned to him, that the weight of the earth keeps increasing by the day, with all the new people that are being born. So, he thought it was pretty impressive that this big ball that we live on keeps getting heavier by the day, but yet stays suspended in thin air. I asked him if he could take a baseball and make it be suspended in thin air. He said he couldn't. So, I asked him what he thought about the earth being suspended in midair and not falling. But then he said that it's just gravity that holds the earth up, and causes the earth to revolve around the sun. Then we started discussing who created gravity, and the people on the earth, and all the animals and fish. And he started telling me about what he was learning in school. And I realized just how much the public schools are now trying to explain away God being the creator of everything seen and unseen. And of course, whichever way you choose to believe, it all takes faith. The question is, how sure are you about what you believe? So, let's get into the next chapter to see how it all began.

He Created It All - From Start to Finish

The Beginning

Genesis 1:1-31

¹*In the beginning God created the heavens and the earth.* ²*Now the earth was formless and empty, darkness was over the surface of the deep, and the Spirit of God was hovering over the waters.*

³*And God said, "Let there be light," and there was light.* ⁴*God saw that the light was good, and he separated the light from the darkness.* ⁵*God called the light "day," and the darkness he called "night." And there was evening, and there was morning—the first day.*

⁶*And God said, "Let there be a vault between the waters to separate water from water."* ⁷*So God made the vault and separated the water under the vault from the water above it. And it was so.* ⁸*God called the vault "sky." And there was evening, and there was morning—the second day.*

⁹*And God said, "Let the water under the sky be gathered to one place, and let dry ground appear." And it was so.* ¹⁰*God*

called the dry ground "land," and the gathered waters he called "seas." And God saw that it was good.

*11*Then God said, "Let the land produce vegetation: seed-bearing plants and trees on the land that bear fruit with seed in it, according to their various kinds." And it was so. *12*The land produced vegetation: plants bearing seed according to their kinds and trees bearing fruit with seed in it according to their kinds. And God saw that it was good. *13*And there was evening, and there was morning—the third day.

*14*And God said, "Let there be lights in the vault of the sky to separate the day from the night, and let them serve as signs to mark sacred times, and days and years, *15*and let them be lights in the vault of the sky to give light on the earth." And it was so. *16*God made two great lights—the greater light to govern the day and the lesser light to govern the night. He also made the stars. *17*God set them in the vault of the sky to give light on the earth, *18*to govern the day and the night, and to separate light from darkness. And God saw that it was good. *19*And there was evening, and there was morning—the fourth day.

*20*And God said, "Let the water teem with living creatures, and let birds fly above the earth across the vault of the sky." *21*So God created the great creatures of the sea and every living thing with which the water teems and that moves about in it, according to their kinds, and every winged bird according to its kind. And God saw that it was good. *22*God blessed them and said, "Be fruitful and increase in number and fill the water in the seas, and let the birds increase on the earth." *23*And there was evening, and there was morning—the fifth day.

²⁴And God said, "Let the land produce living creatures according to their kinds: the livestock, the creatures that move along the ground, and the wild animals, each according to its kind." And it was so. ²⁵God made the wild animals according to their kinds, the livestock according to their kinds, and all the creatures that move along the ground according to their kinds. And God saw that it was good.

²⁶Then God said, "Let us make mankind in our image, in our likeness, so that they may rule over the fish in the sea and the birds in the sky, over the livestock and all the wild animals, and over all the creatures that move along the ground."

²⁷So God created mankind in his own image,

in the image of God, he created them;

male and female, he created them.

²⁸God blessed them and said to them, "Be fruitful and increase in number; fill the earth and subdue it. Rule over the fish in the sea and the birds in the sky and over every living creature that moves on the ground."

²⁹Then God said, "I give you every seed-bearing plant on the face of the whole earth and every tree that has fruit with seed in it. They will be yours for food. ³⁰And to all the beasts of the earth and all the birds in the sky and all the creatures that move along the ground—everything that has the breath of life in it—I give every green plant for food." And it was so.

³¹God saw all that he had made, and it was very good. And there was evening, and there was morning—the sixth day.

Here's the golden nugget I want to point out to you regarding what God's Word says about what He created. Then God said, *"Let us make mankind in our image, in our likeness.*

Genesis 1:26 says directly above, *"Let US make mankind in OUR image, in OUR likeness."*

Who do you think He's referring to? I believe He's talking about Jesus Christ. I wanted to share the very first chapter in the Bible with you, because it may have been a long time for you, since you've read that chapter, or perhaps you have never personally read it for yourself. Maybe you just heard that God created Adam and Eve, and then He stole one of Adams ribs to create Eve, because Adam was lonely. If that's the case, I'd like to persuade you to take a stand regarding believing Genesis chapter 1. What we read in the very first chapter of God's Word, is either true, or it isn't true. And if we want to say that everything was accidentally created, then I want you to think about how ridiculous that sounds. As mentioned earlier, neither you or I could even take 500 pages of white paper with random letters on it, and throw all the pages against the wall creating a big bang. And then pick them all up in a nicely, bound book, to see that they have magically formed themselves to become Webster's dictionary. So, if you're struggling to believe that God created us humans, and all the creatures of the world, then I'm asking you to just believe it. Stop trying to over analyze it all. Just have faith, and believe that the Bible is true. You could analyze it all, until you're blue in the face, but you wouldn't be able to know all the details as to how God the Father, and God the Son created it all. So, you might as well wait until you get to Heaven, to find out all the details. For now, I think we should just trust our Coach, and appreciate all that He has created.

All or Some?

Matthew 25:14-30

14 "Again, it will be like a man going on a journey, who called his servants and entrusted his wealth to them. 15 To one he gave five bags of gold, to another two bags, and to another one bag, each according to his ability. Then he went on his journey. 16 The man who had received five bags of gold went at once and put his money to work and gained five bags more. 17 So also, the one with two bags of gold gained two more. 18 But the man who had received one bag went off, dug a hole in the ground and hid his master's money.

19 "After a long time the master of those servants returned and settled accounts with them. 20 The man who had received five bags of gold brought the other five. 'Master,' he said, 'you entrusted me with five bags of gold. See, I have gained five more.'

21 "His master replied, 'Well done, good and faithful servant! You have been faithful with a few things; I will put you in charge of many things. Come and share your master's happiness!'

[22]"The man with two bags of gold also came. 'Master,' he said, 'you entrusted me with two bags of gold; see, I have gained two more.'

[23]"His master replied, 'Well done, good and faithful servant! You have been faithful with a few things; I will put you in charge of many things. Come and share your master's happiness!'

[24]"Then the man who had received one bag of gold came. 'Master,' he said, 'I knew that you are a hard man, harvesting where you have not sown and gathering where you have not scattered seed. [25]So I was afraid and went out and hid your gold in the ground. See, here is what belongs to you.'

[26]"His master replied, 'You wicked, lazy servant! So, you knew that I harvest where I have not sown and gather where I have not scattered seed? [27]Well then, you should have put my money on deposit with the bankers, so that when I returned I would have received it back with interest.

[28]" 'So take the bag of gold from him and give it to the one who has ten bags. [29]For whoever has will be given more, and they will have an abundance. Whoever does not have, even what they have will be taken from them. [30]And throw that worthless servant outside, into the darkness, where there will be weeping and gnashing of teeth.'

One of my favorite philosophers and business coaches asked the question, "How tall should a tree grow?" I always like to ask people that question. I always remind my kids about that question, because at different times of their lives, or my own life, we can forget the correct answer. So, ask yourself that question. According to the above parable that Jesus spoke, known as the parable of the talents, there's only one correct answer. And the answer to how tall a tree should grow IS NOT

"As tall as it wants." That tree would be considered an underachiever. The correct answer is, "as tall as it can." Anything else would qualify as being less than it can be, as opposed to all that it can be. Unlike trees, we humans have been given the dignity to choose how much of our potential we will live up to. Will we choose to be some of what we can be, or will we choose to become all that we can be? Jesus makes it clear in verse 26, that if we choose to do less than we're capable of, then we're being a wicked and lazy servant. It's no different than the lazy person on the football team or baseball team. Have you ever seen a baseball player hit a ground ball to the short stop, and he barely runs to first base? He's practically walking because he's not willing to put in the extra effort. Then, there's the guy who runs as fast as he can to first base to try and beat the throw. That's the guy the coach is pleased with. That's the guy who has heart. That's the guy who the coach will reward when his contract is up and it's time to reward him with a big, fat, juicy paycheck. Coach Jesus rewards those who give Him their FULL effort.

Review the Highlight Film in Your Mind, Then Move Forward

Have you ever played something that happened in the past, over and over in your mind, until it completely depressed and discouraged you from taking action in the present moment? I think we can all relate to getting paralyzed by failure. But what if you looked at failure as an opportunity to learn from that experience, instead of dwelling on it, and letting it cripple you from moving forward in life? What if there was no such thing as losing or failing, as-long-as you learned something from that experience, and simply took new action with a different approach, and applied what you learned moving forward? Could you feel better about your future if you knew that failure was only temporary and really wasn't failure at all? Jesus wants us to focus on Him, and the future. Because, with Jesus, nothing is ever over. We get to live forever, and our mistakes and sin can only hold us back if we refuse to repent. I learned early on in my walk with Jesus, that the definition of "repent," was to make a 180-degree turn. Which means if you're stealing or lying, turn completely away from doing that, and walk the opposite direction. If you're getting negative thoughts all the time, then you need to turn those thoughts towards the positive and in the opposite direction of the negative.

Right now, you can watch the game highlights in your mind and look at them differently. Instead of focusing on the mistakes, and accepting them as mistakes, you can look at the situation differently with the goal of figuring out what you did wrong, then take the necessary action to do better next time. Think about the power you will have if you can turn away from your mistakes, and correct them by making the necessary adjustments. Have you ever used GPS in your car? If so, then you know that any wrong turn you make, gets corrected by the GPS. It may take a bit longer for you to get to your destination, but you'll still get there because you'll be re-routed. God has His own GPS. It's simply called, "Gods Positioning System." It's powered by His Holy Spirit. So, if you know where you want to go, or what you want to accomplish, you just need to have the faith and trust that His GPS will guide you to where you want to go. Don't have the attitude of being lost with no hope of getting there.

Jesus promised those of us who would believe in Him, that He would send us the promised gift of The Holy Spirit and that He would guide and counsel us. Are you pausing during your times of being lost and discouraged, to ask Him for encouragement and guidance? If not, you can do it at this very moment. Take a minute to ask Him to re-route you to the right road that will lead to accomplishing your dreams. You have 2 choices … you can either quit and get discouraged, or you can pray for guidance and continue, on your journey. Sometimes I'll get so lost, that I just pray to God at that moment wherever I am, and I just say in my mind, "Lord, I am so lost … I have no idea what to do right now. Please help me. I'm so discouraged." And then within minutes, I seem to get some mental, spiritual, and emotional guidance to be re-routed on to the right road. I used to think that my prayers had to be long, but now I know that my prayers can happen at any time, and be any length. If Jesus is always with us, then we should always be able to pray to Him, right? So, look at the game highlights in your mind, and learn what you can do differently moving forward. If you do that, everything will work out just fine.

His Players Never Retire

> Psalm 90:4 *"A thousand years in your sight are like a day that has just gone by, or like a watch in the night."*

As I write these words it's Easter Sunday. It's also my birthday. I just turned 47 years young today. The reason I say young, is because I'm always trying to look at life as the glass being half full rather than half empty. If I say that I'm old, then I'll feel old, and perhaps start to look old. Compared to someone who's 57, I'd say I'm feeling and looking pretty, young. Remember when we talked about how words and thoughts are seeds? I believe that thoughts of feeling, and looking old, will grow into gray hair and wrinkles. Even more important than looking old, is feeling old. When I read the whole Bible, I didn't notice God disqualifying older people from doing great things in His name. But what I did notice in God's Word, was how many of His players were very old when He used them the most. Moses was 80 years old when he spoke to Pharaoh, and delivered the Israelites out of Egypt. He led them to freedom as Pharaoh and the Egyptian army were breathing down their necks. But Moses and the Israelites walked safely through the parted Red Sea, while their enemies were drowned. How about Noah when the flood came, and he and his family, along with all the various creatures of the world, were loaded into the ark, the day the flood began? God's Word says that Noah was 600 years old. How about you? How old are you? Or should I ask you, how young are you, compared to Noah and Moses? When you're being coached by Jesus, you fully understand that you're never too old to fulfill His plans for your life.

You must get it into your mind, heart, and soul, that it's never too late for you to do great things in your life, no matter how old you are. As you can see in Psalm 90:4, a thousand years to God, is like 1 day to us. He operates on a different clock than we do. You may not see a way to victory in your life, but God can turn your situation around in 1 second. He can take you from zero to hero. So, get your fire back. Start believing again. Start looking up instead of down. As-long-as you have a beating heart, you can win. And even if you're heart stopped beating, you could be brought back to life physically according to God's Word. Jesus brought a little girl back to life. He brought Lazarus back to life. The apostles were even able to bring people back to life through His resurrection power. You have been given the same power that Jesus had, and still has at His disposal, when He was healing the blind, and getting the crippled to walk again. He's still doing those same miracles today, and He's using people like you and I to do them. Faith is the key.

HE LOVES GIVING HIS PLAYERS GREAT GIFTS

Luke 11:11-13

> [11] "Which of you fathers, if your son asks for a fish, will give him a snake instead? [12] Or if he asks for an egg, will give him a scorpion? [13] If you then, though you are evil, know how to give good gifts to your children, how much more will your Father in heaven give the Holy Spirit to those who ask him!"

The word "Desire" in the original Latin translation means, "Of the Father."

If there's a righteous dream in your heart that you have always had the desire to fulfill, then God has put that desire in your heart. He wouldn't have put it in you if He wasn't going to give you everything you need to achieve it. I'm asking you to have faith in Him as your Coach. I'm asking you to start believing again. Remember, when you believe you will receive. But when you doubt, you will go without.

God designed us humans to be happy. That's the state that He wants us to be in. Too many of us believe that being broke, and unhappy, equals humility. I myself can sometimes get caught in the lies of Satan, when he tries to deceive me by saying, that God doesn't want me to have a nice house, nice car, or a nice new guitar. But I know that the truth is,

God wants us to be happy. I also know that as-long-as we're not putting those nice things before Him, and as-long-as we're grateful to Him for blessing us with those things, then it brings Him great pleasure to give them to us. We need to give Him our gratitude for them, in the same exact way you would be grateful to your earthly father, if he gave those things to you. But notice how He compares our earthly father's gifts to us, as compared to the gift He gives to us, known as, "The Holy Spirit," to those who ask Him. As we discussed earlier, you and I have been given the same Power that Jesus used to raise the dead, and restore sight to the blind. If God gives you a really nice car to get to work, or to drive your family around in, I'd say that He's given you or me a great gift. But compared to the gift of the Holy Spirit, I'd say the car is the booby prize.

I believe that when someone gives you a gift, they want to know that you appreciate it, and that you're using it. A few days ago, my son cleaned his bedroom out, and he took his big model of the Titanic cruise ship out of his room. It's a perfect replica of the original, before it sank of course. He also took a really, nice utility pocket knife, out of his room, that had his name engraved in the wood on the pocket knife. My wife noticed that the knife was taken out of his room, and asked him about it. My wife's feelings were a bit hurt, because she knew that my son wasn't really into the knife that she gave to him as a gift. Our son obviously didn't want it to be in his bedroom anymore. The point of this story, is that God sees how we feel, about the gifts he has given us. He knows if we're grateful for what He's given us. The secret to being happy and getting more of anything in life, is to live with an attitude of gratitude.

One of my favorite preachers says, "When you praise, you will be raised, but when you complain, you will remain." That's so true in my life. When I'm not grateful for what I've been given, I noticed that the pipeline of gifts, seems to get shut off. I'm not just talking about material gifts, I'm talking about my musical talents start getting stagnant, and I seem to no longer want to play in front of people, or write new songs. When I stop trying to encourage others to follow their dreams, and to never give up, I end up getting discouraged myself. If God gives you any kind of gift, it's so important to not only say that you're grateful for it, but to show that you're grateful for it by using it. As I write these words, I'm in my 7ft X 7ft sound proof Whisper Room. I go in here each morning, to have my coaching sessions with Jesus. I also write and record music in here, so the microphone doesn't pick up the barking of our furry little family members.

As I look in front of me, I see one of my extremely cool Taylor Solid body guitars. When I first bought it with the money Jesus allowed me to make, I was so excited about it, and I played it like a maniac. I still love that guitar, but sometimes when I look at it, I don't really feel that I appreciate it anywhere as much as I used to, the first few days I received it. So, I just took a moment to pause, and to picture in my mind, the day that I bought it for a sweet deal on Craigslist. I remember looking at it in the driveway of the guy I bought it from. It was a beautiful sunny day, and I drove about 45 miles to get it. This guitar should have sold for about $400 dollars more than I paid for it. I remember when he opened the hardshell case and told me how he barely played it, and said, "As you can tell, it still looks and plays like new." At that moment, I thought in my mind, "Thank you Jesus for hooking me up with this great deal!!" I struggle quite often with being grateful, and need to remind myself of what my Coach says will bring me more blessings in life. Is there something or someone in your life who you could be grateful for right now, if you wanted to? If you're feeling discouraged and depressed right now, then taking a few minutes to focus in on one thing or person that you're grateful to God for, will immediately make you happy. It usually works for me, and I believe it will work for you as well.

A Personal Testimony from One of Jesus' Players

2 Peter 1:16-18

> *[16] "For we did not follow cleverly devised stories when we told you about the coming of our Lord Jesus Christ in power, but we were eyewitnesses of his majesty. [17] He received honor and glory from God the Father when the voice came to him from the Majestic Glory, saying, "This is my Son, whom I love; with him I am well pleased." [18] We ourselves heard this voice that came from heaven when we were with him on the sacred mountain."*

Peter, as you may already know, was one of Jesus' original 12 disciples. The word "disciple" simply means, "student of." So, Peter was a student of Jesus. Or one of the players on His team. As we discussed earlier, Peter ended up walking on the water towards Jesus. Peter was also the guy who said he would never let Jesus down, even if everyone else did. But Jesus told him that before the rooster crows, Peter would deny Him not once, but 3 times. Even with Peter denying Jesus 3 times on the day Jesus was crucified, Peter was put back in the game to march toward victory with Jesus. When Peter says in 2 Peter 1:16:16, that he and the other disciples did not follow cleverly devised stories when they told people about the coming of Jesus. But that they were eyewitnesses of His Majesty. So, what do you think? Was Peter lying? He says that he and the others witnessed it with their own eyes, and heard everything with their own ears. Their experience wasn't virtual reality ... they lived it. Peter was sentenced to die by being crucified because of his unwillingness to stop telling and teaching people about Jesus. The reason he was willing to die for his beliefs about Jesus, was because he was there, and he knew it really happened. He saw all the amazing miracles Jesus had performed. Not only that, Peter was able to perform miracles himself, by the power of the Holy Spirit. Peter honored and respected Jesus so much, that he insisted on being crucified upside down. He didn't feel worthy of dying the same way as his Lord and Savior had been put to death. In the court of law, someone is convicted of guilt, if there are 2 witnesses. In the Bible, there are 12 personal accounts, and personal testimonies of what Jesus did. Those personal eyewitness testimonies are all written in the Bible. Have you ever read the whole Bible? If not, then I suggest you start today. Make the decision to not only read the whole Bible, but to go online and to follow a 365 day, or shorter, reading plan to make that happen. It's important that you read all the personal testimonies that give a personal accounting of what Jesus did and said. After all, you're reading the owner's manual for us humans. Don't you want to know all the details of who you are, what you're capable of, and how you were created?

WE ALL HAVE OUR GOOD GAMES AND OUR BAD GAMES

I just received a call from my brother, and he shared with me his thoughts about a fellow Christian, who had been helping him out with something. And then his friend decided that he was done helping him. My brother was feeling a bit upset with his friend, because he stopped helping him with the situation he needed help with. As I was talking to my brother, it had dawned on me that he was forgetting that his friend had already helped him for 2 weeks. I don't want to get into the exact details of how this guy helped my brother, but I will say that it was a pretty, big sacrifice on the part of his friend. I knew my brother was feeling upset with his friend, so I asked him, "How long did you say your friend had helped you?" He said, "He helped me for the last 2 weeks." I told him that his friend was being pretty, generous to help him like that for 2 weeks. He then started to turn his judging of this friend for not continuing to help him, into being grateful for the help that his friend had already given him. I told my brother that perhaps your friend was in a good place spiritually during the 2 weeks he was willing to help you. Maybe now he's struggling with something in his own life, and isn't in the frame of mind to keep helping you. It made me think about this game of life that you and I are in. I look at each day as a different game, inning, quarter, period or set of downs. I like to take things day by day, and when I get the gift of being able to wake up the next morning, then it's a new opportunity, that I have been given to move closer to winning in the game of life. Perhaps my brother's friend was being attacked by the enemy, and was now in need of some help himself. I'm not saying this to judge my brother or his friend, but I'm saying this to make the point that we all need to help our fellow teammates at different times in the game. We need to help each other to get back in the game and win. It's a brand new set of downs, to get the football, and get into the end zone. Or if you're playing baseball, it's a, brand new, chance to be up to bat and drive in the winning run. And in basketball, it would be the player with the ball who has the chance to sink a 3 pointer through the hoop as the buzzer goes off to complete the comeback victory. We're all going to have good games and bad games. We may not be undefeated, but our Coach is. And in the end, we end up winning the game. Period!!

Savor the Sweet Victories

After the New England Patriots won the Super Bowl in 2017. I re-watched the highlights on YouTube quite a few times. I heard the news stations talking about it, and the music stations talking about it. I watched the parade that was held for the Patriots. I was savoring the victory because it was so inspiring and encouraging to me, that it translated into my own life. It reminded me that I too, could come from behind and win no matter what the odds. We're so willing to relive other people's victories in their lives, especially when it comes to a sporting event. But, very rarely, do we relive our own personal victories, because they're not posted on YouTube or being shown on the news. So, here's the solution to relive and remember your victories throughout your life.

In-order to relive your own personal victories, you must first pull out your journal and think about all the victories you can remember having in your life. If you don't have a journal, you can simply jot down the notes on your phone or pull out a piece of paper. It's easy to forget about the victories you had in your life. So that's why I'd like you to do this exercise with me. I want you to go back to kindergarten if you need to. Write down any victory you have ever had, even if it was winning a game of dodge ball in gym class. Maybe there was a bully in your class who you were competing with in dodge ball, and you threw the ball at him and nailed him with the ball in that extremely sensitive area. Or maybe you threw the ball at his stomach and knocked the wind out of him. I'm not trying to be politically correct here. Jesus wasn't politically correct, and David wasn't being politically correct when he chopped Goliath's head off, and held it in the air to taunt the enemies of God.

The "Hell City Demons," will push your face in your own defeat. They're not worried about your feelings. They want you to feel so defeated that you'll give up completely and go kill yourself. That's the truth. And sadly, enough, there are many people every day, who become so defeated and discouraged, that they take their own life. If they could have been reminded of their victories in life, they would have had renewed hope and meaning in their life. They might not have decided to check out of the game of life. But that's exactly what happens when you completely forget the fact that you have won different battles in your life that mattered to you or someone you love. Do you know of anyone in your life right now who could benefit from you reminding them of any victories or good things that you have witnessed in their life? If so, I would like you to give them a call, or shoot them an email, to remind them of it. Sometimes a quick little reminder could prevent them from checking out of the game. But if you're in a place right now where you're considering checking out of the game early, then I want you to know that you're winning right now by simply reading this book. You wouldn't be reading this book if there wasn't any fight left in you. God has some great plans in store for you!

Jeremiah 29:11

> [11] *"For I know the plans I have for you," declares the Lord, "plans to prosper you and not to harm you, plans to give you hope and a future."*

Did you hear that? God has plans for you my friend!! Plans to prosper you and plans to give you hope and a future. So, don't ever give up! Now go out into this world and encourage as many people as you can to never ever give up as well.

What Station Are You Tuned Into?

Have you ever been flipping through the radio stations, or changing the tv stations on your remote control, and either heard nothing but lame and depressing songs, or saw very depressing tv shows? I'm pretty sure you have. It's easy to get into a funk. That's why professional athletes always listen to some uplifting, empowering music, or watch something very powerful before the game starts. Do you remember when I told you about my fire walking experience, and how I was taught to do a power move to get myself into a peak state where I could smash the cover off the baseball? To do the fire walk, I was also taught to say out, loud, the words, "Cool Moss, Cool Moss," as I was walking over the burning hot coals with my bare feet. The reason I did that is because, if I were to say out, loud, "Burning Hot Coals, Burning Hot Coals," that's what I would have been focusing in on. I was successful doing the fire walk, because I was tuned into "The Cool Moss Station." The way to control the outcome of the game is to take control of what station you tune into.

He Chooses the Rejects

1 Samuel 16:7

> *But the LORD said to Samuel, "Do not consider his appearance or his height, for I have rejected him. The LORD does not look at the things people look at. People look at the outward appearance, but the LORD looks at the heart."*

What an awesome Scripture to describe how Jesus picks the players to be on His team. Samuel was the prophet whom God chose to recruit the next King of Israel. King Saul was blowing it big time, and God needed to find His new franchise quarterback, who could lead His team to victory. Samuel was told, by God that he needs to ignore the things that everyone else would look at and to make the decision as to who their next king should be. He told him to ignore how he looks, and to ignore how tall he is. Most professional sports teams wouldn't ignore all the other qualities, even if the player had great skills and stats, because they would say that the athlete has done great in College of High School, but in the big leagues they couldn't make it. As 1 Samuel 16:7 says, *"Jesus looks at the heart."* His players must be whole heartedly committed to Him. I'll never forget how good it felt to know that my younger brother and my cousin, told me that several years after I had left Junior High, my coach when I was on the basketball team and softball team, would always tell them the story of a kid he coached who wasn't the biggest, he wasn't the strongest, and he wasn't the fastest, but he tried with all his heart. And here I am, over 30 years later, still carrying his encouraging words that he said about my heart for winning. Coach Macal was a great coach, and that's why I insisted on putting him as the coach in the song "Halftime," that I told you about in the beginning of this book. He gave me a starting spot on the team when most other coaches wouldn't even have given me a chance. I wanted to give even more effort, during the games, out of gratitude that Coach Macal gave me a chance to be on his team. How much more should you and I want to give to Coach Jesus for choosing us to be on His team? When He chose you, He looked at your heart, and He knew you had what it takes to be in His starting lineup. He believes in you, and He wants you to believe in Him as your coach.

HE DOESN'T WANT YOU TO GET BUFF AT THE BUFFET

>John 4:34 *"My food," said Jesus, "is to do the will of him who sent me and to finish his work."*

Have you ever heard someone say that they're getting buff? I may be dating myself, because I'm not sure if that's still the way today's young generation describes getting muscular and lean. But in my high school days, that's the way we described it. I used to tell people who hadn't seen me in a while, and noticed that I put on some weight, that I was getting "buff at the buffet." In other words, I looked fat. My younger brother was notorious for asking me if I'd been working out, every time he wouldn't see me in a while, and it was obvious to him that I gained some weight. As I write this chapter, I'm getting back on track with my healthy eating, and consistently working out. For me it's a constant struggle and temptation to eat foods that are bad for me. In John 4:34 Jesus says that His food is to do the will of Him who sent Him and to finish His work. Until I understood what Jesus was saying there, I didn't realize that doing God's will would satisfy my hunger for eating bad food. Have you ever heard that Snickers candy bar commercial where it says, "Snickers satisfies you," and then you instantly want to go and eat a Snickers bar? That's the exact same thing that Jesus is telling us. He's eating soul food. And it's very satisfying. He's getting fed and nourished spiritually by doing His Father's work.

When you or I are busy doing any kind of work, we're usually too busy to be munching on a bunch of food that's bad for us. We're feeling fully alive and energized and we just don't think about eating constantly.

In the Bible, there's a word called "Gluttony." I don't know if you've ever used that word, or heard it being used. But it's basically someone who eats way, too much. So, they're called a "Glutton." What if we were gluttons when it comes to feasting on God's spiritual buffet, instead of eating foods that will make us fat, discouraged and depressed? Our lives would change, completely wouldn't they? What I always do when I notice that I'm getting off track with my health and fitness, is to immediately cut out all sugar except from fruit & honey which I use for my organic coffee. I also cut out all dairy, except the little amount of creamer that I pour into my coffee. I realize that there's so many different eating plans, and work out plans, that you or I could follow, but I'm just sharing with you what I usually do. I rarely eat red meat. And when I eat meat, it's usually on my once a week cheat meal where I can have dessert or whatever else I want to eat. I was reading, recently online, what two of the oldest living people on earth credit their long life to … they both said, "it's because they ate eggs every day." But don't the doctors say that the high cholesterol from the egg yolk will give you a heart attack? It's just so hard to figure out what physical eating plan is best for us. But what Jesus is saying is that His eating plan is a spiritual eating plan. He did not go around preaching to people that they need to cut out the carbs and eat more protein. But, since we are on-the-subject of carbs and protein, I like to eat a lot of low fat beans because they have a ton of protein, and this helps me to stay away from needing to eat a bunch of animal protein or animal fat. I'd like to give a big disclaimer here. I'm not a nutritionist and I'm not telling you how to eat, or what to eat. I'm letting you know what eating plan Jesus recommends. He recommends soul food that nourishes your body and soul. He wants us to stop getting buff at the buffet. If you're fat right now, be honest with yourself and do something about it. It may be tough to do at first, but each day you eat His soul food, you'll find it easier and easier to resist the temptation of eating the foods that are making you fat.

He Wants You to Walk Your Talk

Proverbs 14:23 *"All hard work brings a profit, but mere talk leads only to poverty."*

Luke 13:31-33

31 At that time some Pharisees came to Jesus and said to him, "Leave this place and go somewhere else. Herod wants to kill you."

32 He replied, "Go tell that fox, 'I will keep on driving out demons and healing people today and tomorrow, and on the third day I will reach my goal.' 33 In any case, I must press on today and tomorrow and the next day—for surely no prophet can die outside Jerusalem!

Have you ever met someone who's all talk and no action? Sadly, I have had times in my life that I would describe myself as that guy. Writing this book is something I talked about doing for many years. But I'm finally doing it. If you're one of the people who fits into the "All Talk" category, it's not too late to "Walk the Talk."

Writing a book is hard work that requires consistency and commitment. I've been writing songs, pretty much, since I've been 3 years old and have found that many of my best songs were written in about 1 hour. That included the music and the lyrics.

In Proverbs 14:23, *God is saying that "All hard work brings a profit, but mere talk leads only to poverty."* I don't think He's just referring to financial poverty. I think He's talking about poverty in every aspect of our lives. Self-esteem is one of the most important areas to prosper in. To esteem is to respect, or hold up in high regard. So, to have self-esteem is to respect yourself. How can you or I respect ourselves, if we're all talk and no action? I used to struggle with telling everyone, including my wife and kids, everything that I was going to do. But then a year would pass by and then 2 years. And all that was accomplished was me saying what I was going to do, instead of doing what I said I would do. Aren't you happy that Jesus did what He said He would do?

Jesus knew what He needed to do, and He took immediate action. Not only that, but in Luke 13:31-33, Jesus said that He would keep taking, action, until He reached His goal. He knew that He needed to reach His goal of being crucified within Jerusalem. So, He took care of business. His goal was to be crucified on the cross, die, and then be raised back to life on the third day so that you and I could also be raised from the dead and be with Him in Heaven for all eternity. He knew what the goal was. I don't think you or I could possibly have a goal that would be harder to take action on, like Jesus' goal of dying on the cross, so that you and I could be forgiven. Can you? Do you know what your goals are in life? If not, I want you to take some time right now, and give some very serious thought as to what you want in life. I know how difficult it can be to make a decision regarding what you want out of life, but once I decided exactly what I wanted, I felt relieved ... I was no longer drifting in life. You can't hit a bullseye if you don't know where it is, can you? Once you make a decision and commit to taking action, then victory will be assured. But we must continue to seek coaching from Jesus.

He Wants You to Know the Rules of His Game

> Proverbs 14:12 *"There is a way that appears to be right, but in the end, it leads to death."*

What if there was no dividing line in the road letting cars know to stay in their own lane? What would happen if two cars were driving down the road, at the same time, in opposite directions, without that dividing line in the road? You guessed it. They would probably crash into each other head on and die. That's why all great coaches want you to know the rules of the game. They want you to know where the boundaries are. We need to know when we're out of bounds. We need to know, when we hit a ball in baseball, if it's a fair ball or a foul ball. Otherwise, we could think that we're winning the game, and scoring, when we're, really, not winning. Instead, we're losing without even knowing it. In Proverbs 14:12, God says, *"There is a way that appears to be right, but in the end, it leads to death."* I don't know about you, but I don't want to be fooling myself, that what I'm doing is good, only to find out that it's going to kill me. It reminds me of a story you may have already heard about. It's a story about a frog being boiled in a pot of water. The flame starts out at a lower temperature, and then in very small increments, the heat gets turned up. But the frog doesn't notice it because the water he's in appears to be ok temperature wise at the time. The water temperature keeps getting hotter and eventually gets to the boiling point. But the change in temperature was too incrementally small for him to notice, so he stays in the boiling water, and ends up getting boiled to death. Just as we need to know the rules, we also need to know the life-threatening details in our lives.

Drifting Down the River of Life

This next story is about a guy who was drifting in a boat near Niagara Falls. It was a beautiful day, and the sun was shining. The breeze was just right, and there was barely any humidity. So, the man decided to drift and take a nap. He was from out of town on vacation, and he didn't really know the river very well. He didn't see the warning signs letting him know that he was approaching Niagara Falls, because he was taking a nap on this beautiful paradise like day. As his boat started drifting dangerously close to the point of going over Niagara Falls, the sight seers who had come to visit the Falls, were looking at the boat, and noticed that there was a man in the boat who was either dead, or asleep. The people started yelling to get the guy's attention, but the guy didn't respond, or wake up, until a few moments before going down the Falls in his boat. The outcome wasn't good. His boat crashed to the bottom of the Falls, and the man died. It was too late for anyone to rescue him.

Have you ever found yourself drifting in life and thinking life was all good? Maybe you got married 20 years ago, you said your vows to love your wife and to always protect her. But as time passed by, you ended up drifting away from that commitment. Maybe when your kids were young, you were going to church on a regular basis and that meant that your kids were going to church as well. But when they started getting older, you stopped going to church very much, and your kids ended up hanging out with the wrong crowd instead of having friends who would help them in their walk with Jesus. I'm not saying, "you have to go to church every week to raise your kids to be great Christians." But the more we all get around "The Word," and other Christians, the more we will be encouraged and inspired by their genuine friendship and example. If we will consistently do this, we will all benefit as Christians.

His Players Don't Drink Gatorade

John 4:11-13

> *[11]"Sir," the woman said, "you have nothing to draw with and the well is deep. Where can you get this living water? [12]Are you greater than our father Jacob, who gave us the well and drank from it himself, as did also his sons and his livestock?"*
>
> *[13]Jesus answered, "Everyone who drinks this water will be thirsty again, [14]but whoever drinks the water I give them will never thirst. Indeed, the water I give them will become in them a spring of water welling up to eternal life."*

In the Scripture above, Jesus is talking to a woman at a well. He was basically talking to her about the quality of the water in the well. He told her that He can give her water that will make her never thirst again and it will become an internal spring of water welling up to eternal life.

Have you ever seen the movie called "The Water Boy" with Adam Sandler? If not, then it's another movie I highly recommend. It's extremely funny. Adam Sandler plays the water boy in the movie and his job is to make sure that all the players, on the football team, are well hydrated. He's so passionate and excited to make sure they're well prepared for the game that the mention of Gatorade, to "The Water Boy," really gets him upset. Jesus feels the same way when it comes to giving His players the best water to drink. He cares so much about us that He gives us living water. The thirst, Jesus is referring to, is our thirst for peace and contentment in our lives and to be at peace in our souls. The living water, Jesus is referring to, is His Word in His Playbook, known as the Bible. Are you reading it? It's not very hard to understand it. The enemy wants us to think that it's way too complicated for the ordinary average person to read and understand. He's lying!!

> Ephesians 5:26 *²⁶to make her holy, cleansing her by the washing with water through the word,*

He Says You Can Predict Your Own Victory

Growing up, as a kid, I played and loved baseball. I was a huge Cubs fan and my dad grew up being an even bigger Cubs fan than I was. In case you didn't know, last year the Cubs won the World Series, and ended a 108-year drought. The last time they won the World Series was 1908. We talked about how Jesus says, that according to your faith, it will be done for you right? I believe that He meant that, even for winning the World Series. The last time the Cubs were in the World Series was 1945. Up until 1945, they were one of the most successful baseball teams in America, with a 5475-4324 record. That's a .559 winning percentage, which included 51 winning seasons, 16 pennants, and World Series games that they would compete in. They ended up winning two World Series titles, and 6 Championship titles in that time span. BUT their winning hit a brick wall in game 4 of the 1945 World Series. You should google the whole story because it's so interesting that entire books and documentaries have been made about it. The Cubs' history fits right into what Jesus said about "believing" being the key to receiving. As mentioned, their winning ways ended in 1945 of game 4 when a local tavern owner bought two tickets to the game … one for himself and one for his pet Billy goat. He was a major Cubs' fan, and when he went to the game, the ushers wouldn't let the goat in. The goat was a pet, and the owner thought he'd bring his pet goat as a good luck mascot for the Cubs. The situation was brought all the way up to the owner of the Cubs and he said that the goat couldn't come into the game because it stunk. They said the owner of the goat could come into the game, but not the goat. The owner was upset, so legend has it, he threw up his arms, and said, "The Cubs 'ain't gonna' win no more … the Cubs will never win a World Series again so long as the goat is not allowed in Wrigley Field." What followed next, after the proclaimed curse on the Cubs, is incredible. The Cubs went on to lose game 4, and then the next two games, to lose the World Series. Very quickly, after the loss, the owner of the goat sent a letter to the owner of the Cubs saying, "Who stinks now?" And that was the beginning of the curse. The Chicago media quickly, picked up the story, and spread the news of the Billy goat curse. It became a much bigger story than the Cubs' history and reputation for winning. Every time the Cubs would get close to going to the World Series, the whole team, and the entire city, started talking about the curse of the Billy goat. This caused them all to no longer believe they could win because of the curse. They would talk about it in a joking manner, but at the same time, they would wonder if it was true. The reporters would ask the owner of the Cubs, the coaches, and all the players about the curse. That was the main story. It was quite amusing, to watch, but very frustrating to see the Cubs choke every time they would get close to victory.

I remember watching all the games growing up with my dad, and whenever the Cubs were losing, my dad would say, "It's over, they're not going to come back." Or, if they had the lead, and someone on the other team got a hit, my dad would say, "That's it, they're going to blow it, that's what they always do." Not only was my dad's faith in the Cubs weak, but it also made my faith in them weak as well. My dad would repeatedly, throughout my years of watching the Cubs' game with him, say, "I'll be dead before the Cubs win the World Series." Sadly, my dad was right. He truly believed that he would die before seeing the Cubs win the World Series. You need to understand how into the Cubs my dad was. Even though he didn't believe in them, he was following them every season. He would listen to WGN sports radio and hear all the other Cubs' doubters discussing every year how the Cubs were going to choke again. My dad would also read all the articles about the Cubs in the sports section of the Chicago Sun Times. He was hooked. I feel like

I just wrote a book about the Cubs, but it's one of the most powerful examples of how faith and belief, opens or shuts, the door to victory. .

Numbers 13:33 *"We even saw giants there, the descendants of Anak. Next to them we felt like grasshoppers, and that's what they thought, too!"*

Like Jesus said, *"According to your faith it will be done for you."* The rest of the story is history. In 2016, they finally realized there was no curse and they won the World Series. Their new players, coaches, and executive leadership didn't grow up believing in the Billy goat curse being on the Cubs. They simply believed that they could win the World Series. I'd like to believe that my dad was watching the game in Heaven with all the other die-hard Cubs' fans. What lie, or lies, does the enemy have you believing?

All His Players Have Eternal Life Insurance

Treasures in Heaven

Matthew 6:19-21

> [19]"Do not store up for yourselves treasures on earth, where moths and vermin destroy, and where thieves break in and steal. [20] But store up for yourselves treasures in heaven, where moths and vermin do not destroy, and where thieves do not break in and steal. [21] For where your treasure is, there your heart will be also."

Most people get excited about having a life insurance policy because they'll be able to leave plenty of money to their wife and kids … I'm one of those people. I want to know that when I go to be with Jesus in Heaven, that my family is well taken care of financially. Having a ton of bills, and stressing out about how to pay the electric bill or mortgage, can take away a large portion of happiness in anyone's life. I know that from personal experience. I want to make earth as close to Heaven for my family as I can. I want to make sure that I've built a financial wall around my family that the enemy cannot penetrate. I don't know about you, but the words "Stress" and "Heaven," seem to mix like oil, and water.

In Matthew 6:19-21, Jesus is telling us that we need to work on our Heavenly life insurance plan. He's not saying that we need to be legalistic and earn our way to Heaven. But if you'll notice in verse 21, He's saying that where your treasure is, there your heart will be also. He's wanting us to make sure that we understand how important it is to know where we consider our treasure to be. Is it in your job, your car, your house, guitars, diamond rings or your Rolex? Or maybe it's in the hobby that you're passionate about. I don't know about you, but I often think about how hard it is to get excited about something I can't see or have never visited before. A picture says a thousand words. A video says even more. When I'm thinking of buying a new guitar, or music equipment, I look at reviews online. I look at pictures or watch YouTube videos seeing someone else using it. When it comes to Heaven, you or I don't get to see travel brochures, like we do, when going to a resort in Maui. BUT, we do have God's Word which describes Heaven in great detail. It also tells us how to get there. The way you and I can store up treasure for ourselves in Heaven, is to do what our Coach says, to the best of our abilities. The next chapter tells us exactly how we can store up treasure for ourselves in Heaven, without being legalistic.

The Greatest Commandment

Matthew 22:34-40

> ³⁴Hearing that Jesus had silenced the Sadducees, the Pharisees got together. ³⁵One of them, an expert in the law, tested him with this question: ³⁶"Teacher, which is the greatest commandment in the Law?"
>
> ³⁷Jesus replied: "Love the Lord your God with all your heart and with all your soul and with all your mind.' ³⁸This is the first and greatest commandment. ³⁹And the second is like it: 'Love your neighbor as yourself.' ⁴⁰All the Law and the Prophets hang on these two commandments."

I used to complicate what Jesus expects from me. But when I really understood the above Scripture, I finally realized that making Jesus proud of me, was all about loving Him with everything I am. To lay it all on the line for Him and for His people, as well as those who were not yet His people. And who are His people? Are they the neighbors who live on your street, or are they people who you can meet anywhere in the world? I believe He's talking about anyone we meet. In this next Scripture, Jesus gives us the rules on how we can love our neighbor as we love ourselves.

Matthew 25:37-40

> ^{37}"Then the righteous will answer him, 'Lord, when did we see you hungry and feed you, or thirsty and give you something to drink? ^{38}When did we see you a stranger and invite you in, or needing clothes and clothe you? ^{39}When did we see you sick or in prison and go to visit you?'
>
> ^{40}"The King will reply, 'Truly I tell you, whatever you did for one of the least of these brothers and sisters of mine, you did for me.'

What an incredible Scripture!! In sports, we call this the fundamentals. The basic skills we need in-order to win. As a Christian, Jesus just gave us the fundamentals of winning as a Christian and storing up treasures in Heaven. We simply need to love others by being there for them and meeting their needs. There's nothing complicated about that right?

The Blue Tour Bus

My family and I had been living in the Nashville, Tennessee area at the time, and as mentioned earlier, we became, "The Real-Life Brady Bunch Meets the Partridge Family Gone Country." But we were missing one thing ... a bus. I don't know if you've ever seen an episode of "The Partridge Family" tv show, but if you have, then you most likely know that they traveled around in a groovy looking multi-colored converted school bus to most of their gigs, unless they were flying. My family needed a tour bus to do the same thing. The only problem was that we were barely getting by financially at the time. I felt that we needed one, right away, in-order to take us to the next level with our musical journey. I was talking to my wife about it and told her that we need to get one right away. I told her that it's the missing piece to what we're doing. I also told her that we could get musical sponsors, if we had a tour bus, because it would be like a moving billboard that would be an advertisement for our sponsors. I remember it like it was yesterday. After telling my wife all my reasons as to why we needed a tour bus, she said, "Where are you going to find it, on Craigslist? And I bet it will be blue, right? And under $10,000 dollars." I told her, "YES," and that I BELIEVED we would find it on Craigslist. Then she said, "Even if you find it on Craigslist, how are we going to pay for it?" Now the reason this is such an amazing story, is because we already had a blog, and a "Blue Tour Bus Logo" was on our blog. So, I told her, "Let me just check Craigslist in the morning and we'll see what we can find." It was already late, and we were both ready to get some sleep.

So, the next morning I woke up and had my coffee. And while I'm drinking my coffee, I typed in "Tour bus" on Craigslist." Lo and behold, I see a local guy selling a 40-foot long, blue tour bus. It looked exactly like the logo we had on our blog/website. The guy was asking $10,000 for it. I immediately went to get my wife to tell her she's not going to believe this. She came over to my computer screen, and couldn't believe her eyes. I picked up the phone right away to ask the guy if he still had the tour bus. I told him I'd like to come and see it right away. So, we all went out there to see it. Me, my wife, our dog "Presley," and all 6 kids. It was exactly what we were looking for. It was even classified as a vehicle that you didn't have to have your CDL to drive it, which meant that I could be the driver even without having a CDL. I told the guy who was selling the bus, that I wanted it, and asked him if he would finance it for us. He said he would do it, so I gave him $500 as our first payment, and the rest is history. We ended up getting the tour bus wrap sponsored, which was worth over $20,000 dollars. We also ended up getting sponsorship deals with some of the greatest guitar companies, music gear, and accessory companies in the world and ended up putting their logos on the bus.

Matthew 6:33

> [33] *"But seek first his kingdom and his righteousness, and all these things will be given to you as well.* [34] *Therefore do not worry about tomorrow, for tomorrow will worry about itself. Each day has enough trouble of its own."*

Jesus says, in the Scripture above, that if we seek Him and His Kingdom first, we don't need to worry, because He's going to give us everything we need. Do you believe that? If so, get ready for victory in your life. Get ready to take action on those dreams that you didn't think were possible. Get ready for your broken dreams to be put back together. Get ready for your hopes and dreams to be resurrected. You have a Coach that guarantees your victory when you get to know Him, and His "Game Changing Playbook for Your Comeback!!!!" Now get back in the game, and play to win!!!!!

How To Find His Personalized Game Plan for Your Comeback

CONGRATULATIONS!! You've made it into the end zone of this book. That means you're not a quitter!! I believe that you read this book for a reason. And that reason is for you to make one of the greatest personal comebacks in the history of the world. I look forward to hearing your stories of victory. Below is the game plan that Jesus revealed to me through His Word. My hope, prayer, and belief is that the same will happen for you. Victory is guaranteed, "IF" you execute "HIS" game plan consistently.

Jeremiah 29:11-13

> *[11] For I know the plans I have for you," declares the Lord, "plans to prosper you and not to harm you, plans to give you hope and a future. [12] Then you will call on me and come and pray to me, and I will listen to you. [13] You will seek me and find me when you seek me with all your heart.*

By now, you hopefully understand, that He has a plan for your life, and that you can trust that His plan for your life will work. I wrote this book because I wanted to help others to overcome defeat in their lives, just as I have been able to do so in my own life, thanks to being introduced to "The Greatest Coach of All Time." And of course, above all, He's my personal Lord and Savior, who laid down His life for me. He's done the same thing for you. I'm going to show you how I found His personalized game plan for my comeback. I believe this plan will lead you to finding His personalized game plan for your comeback as well.

1. Let Him be your Coach, by surrendering your own game plan, and start believing in Him and His Playbook known as "The Bible." John 3:16, *[16]"For God so loved the world that he gave his one and only Son, that whoever BELIEVES in him shall not perish but have eternal life."* You need to believe in Him if He's going to be your Coach. Romans 10:9 If you confess with your mouth that Jesus is Lord and believe in your heart that God raised him from the dead, you will be saved.

2. Get to know His playbook, and put it into practice. John 8:31-32, *[31] To the Jews who had believed him, Jesus said, "If you hold to my teaching, you are really my disciples.[32] Then you will know the truth, and the truth will set you free."*

3. FORGIVE yourself, and others, by having DAILY strength and strategy sessions with Him through prayer. BUT make sure you have forgiven, from your heart, anyone you know you have not forgiven, including yourself. Otherwise, He says that He will not forgive you. This is perhaps the most important part of being coached by Jesus. SPEAK WITH HIM DAILY.

4. Matthew 6:5-15

   [5]"And when you pray, do not be like the hypocrites, for they love to pray standing in the synagogues and on the street corners to be seen by others. Truly I tell you, they have received their reward in full. [6]But when you pray, go into your room, close the door, and pray to your Father, who is unseen. Then your Father, who sees what is done in secret, will reward you. [7]And when you pray, do not keep on babbling like pagans, for they think they will be heard

because of their many words. ⁸Do not be like them, for your Father knows what you need before you ask him.

⁹"This, then, is how you should pray:

'Our Father in heaven,

hallowed be your name,

¹⁰your kingdom come,

your will be done,

on earth as it is in heaven.

¹¹Give us today our daily bread.

¹²And forgive us our debts,

as we also have forgiven our debtors.

¹³And lead us not into temptation,

but deliver us from the evil one.'

¹⁴For if you forgive other people when they sin against you, your Heavenly Father will also forgive you. ¹⁵But if you do not forgive others their sins, your Father will not forgive your sins.

5. Be at the team meetings as much as you can. As Christians, we need to be encouraged by being around other members on the team. Otherwise it's easy to feel like you're in the game alone. Have you ever heard of a Christian Hermit? Neither have I. Even though Jesus is always with you, He wants you to be around other Christians so you can be encouraged and

experience His presence with other believers and players on the team. With Jesus, there's power in numbers. Jesus says in Matthew *18:19-20, 19"Again, truly I tell you that if two of you on earth agree about anything they ask for, it will be done for them by my Father in Heaven. ²⁰For where two or three gather in My name, there am I with them."* Get in a non-legalistic, Bible based church, and go as often as you can. Jesus doesn't give out attendance awards, so don't base your righteousness by boasting about going to church every Sunday and never missing a service. Do your absolute best to be there, as much as you can, because being there will help you and your family to stay encouraged and to keep your faith strong.

6. Never quit His Team by making sure you wear the Team Uniform every day. The team uniform is otherwise known as "The Full Armor of God." This is the last step in making sure you find and execute Jesus' personalized game plan for your miraculous comeback.

Ephesians 6:10-17

> *¹⁰ Finally, be strong in the Lord and in his mighty power. ¹¹ Put on the full armor of God, so that you can take your stand against the devil's schemes. ¹² For our struggle is not against flesh and blood, but against the rulers, against the authorities, against the powers of this dark world and against the spiritual forces of evil in the heavenly realms. ¹³ Therefore put on the full armor of God, so that when the day of evil comes, you may be able to stand your ground, and after you have done everything, to stand. ¹⁴ Stand firm then, with the belt of truth buckled around your waist, with the breastplate of righteousness in place, ¹⁵ and with your feet fitted with the readiness that comes from the gospel of peace. ¹⁶ In addition to all this, take up the shield of faith, with which you can extinguish all the flaming arrows of*

> *the evil one. ⁱ⁷ Take the helmet of salvation and the sword of the Spirit, which is the word of God.*

You now have, "The Greatest Coach of All Time," coaching you. And, hopefully, you have His "Game Changing Playbook for Your Comeback." If you don't own His Playbook known as "The Bible," you can go to: <u>http://GreatestCoachOfAllTimeBook.com</u> and receive your free electronic version that you can either download to your iPhone, Android, Tablet or Computer. I believe in you and so does Jesus. Get back in the game and play the second half like the 2-minute warning! Lay it all on the line. Cuz it ain't ever over, at Halftime!!